Programming a REAL Internet Site with ASP and HTML

A Science & Technology serial book by Marcelo Bosque.

Programming a REAL Internet Site with ASP and HTML

Book I: HTML and Basic ASP

Includes the source code of a REAL (and still working) on-line page. Readers can also download it from the Web.

A different approach to the study of Active Server Pages and Hypertext Markup Language for students and professionals.

Marcelo Bosque

iUniverse, Inc.
New York Lincoln Shanghai

Programming a REAL Internet Site with ASP and HTML
Book I: HTML and Basic ASP

iUniverse, Inc.

For information address:
iUniverse
2021 Pine Lake Road, Suite 100
Lincoln, NE 68512
www.iuniverse.com

Images and Illustrations by Marcelo Bosque

ISBN: 0-595-27176-6

Printed in the United States of America

To Mary

EPIGRAPH

If all the world's a stage, life must be a play.

Play it again, Sam. The play's the thing

(The author, paraphrasing the bard & Casablanca)

CONTENTS

Other works from the Author xiii

Foreword xv

Preface xvii

Acknowledgements xix

Introduction: Why is this book different? xxi

Part I

What do I do? Choosing a subject and designing the site 1

Chapter 1

Choosing the thematic 3

Chapter 2

What does the customer want? 7

Chapter 3

Starting the site: Preliminary tasks 13

Chapter 4

What do I place in the main page? 17

Chapter 5

When do we start with HTML? 21

How do we program an HTML file? 22

Chapter 6

Now that I know HTML, how do I set up a page? 26

Setting up the language of the page..28

Telling the browser which set of characters must be used 29

Configuring the generator program: 29

Writing a title for the page 29

Chapter 7

How do I do to write text and insert the images? 32

Changing the background color 33

Starting and finishing a paragraph 34

How to give format to a text: 35

Inserting images:...37

Creating tables 38

Writing comments 41

How to place a hyperlink:..42

Chapter 8

Suppose I want to change ALL the fonts of the site at the same
    time…Could I make it? 44

What is a CSS file for?:...44

Creating classes..45

How to enable the CSS file: 48

Chapter 9

Can I make the main page now? 50

Chapter 10

Tell me how to go on with the main page of the site 55

Summary:...60

Chapter 11

Now that I've done the inner part of my main page, I need a menu.
    How do I do it? 61

Creating a standard file to place information in it: 71

Part II

**A small step for the customer, a big leap for the
    programmer** 73

Chapter 12

Nothing is as easy as it seems 75

Part III
Time for ASP 81
Chapter 13
Asp, Asp, What's that? 83
Introduction to Asp 83
What is a database? 84
Why do we need ASP in our page? 84
The ASP itself 87
Chapter 14
Asp Syntax 92
First steps in ASP: 92
How to place text in a ASP page: 92
Publishing an ASP file in the Web 94
ASP usual structures: 98
ASP Environment Variables 102
Opening Databases 103
Chapter 15
Using Databases 106
Storing data on-line 115

Epilogue 127
Appendix 129
About the Author 145

OTHER WORKS FROM THE AUTHOR

Books

From Science & Technology Serial

Understanding 99% of Artificial Neural Networks: Introduction & Tricks

From Self-Entertainment Serial

Shakespeare's Thematic Puzzles!: Includes crossword puzzles, riddles and word search games based in the works of the bard.

Thematic Puzzles!: Includes puzzles about motion pictures, actors, music, writers, Internet, books, American Presidents, computers…etc.

Images, Paintings and Sculptures

The author's visual arts page can be found at http://marcellux.tripod.com.

If you liked any of the images used as front covers of the books, you can find and download them there. You will also find some free gifts to visitors as Calendars and Seasons' Greetings cards.

FOREWORD

This book is a member of my science & technology serial.

The work is divided in two books: The first one talks about the preliminary matters you have to deal with when you need to develop a new Internet Site. It shows you how to program using the HTML language and the basics of ASP. In the second book, we will discuss the ASP programming language deeply.

I'd like to tell you that I did these pages based in a new approach: I asked many of my students about the facts they would like to see (and read) in a programming book. The answers given by them were used as the basic premises to make this work.

This book was not thought to be as a compendium of the knowledge. Most of the guides about HTML and ASP give you all the instructions with all the options you've got to work. The results are "bricks".

I use to call a "brick" to a book that has so many pages and is so tedious to learn that people buy it, read the first chapters, and then place it in the bookshelf.

As a matter of fact, I don't pretend to make a decorative object, but a useful tool for the students and programmers, so I decided to make the sacrifice of all the useless or unusual clauses, in order to do a flexible and readable work. My apologies for the ones who are expecting a complete erudite tractate, but my intention is to make something easy to understand, not an encyclopedia…

Finally, let me tell you that while I was doing it, I have enjoyed myself and I have also learnt a lot about the subject. I expect that at least a part of that fun and knowledge could be transmitted to the readers.

PREFACE

Our remedies oft in ourselves do lie

(William Shakespeare)

I think that this quote from the bard is valid when we speak about Internet and its sites: Many of the problems the programmers face can't be solved using just the standard knowledge. The solution must be obtained using their creativity and internal strength.

We must have this thing in clear: In order to be a good programmer you need to get people who could be able to find the answers in themselves.

ACKNOWLEDGEMENTS

I'd like to thank my students and all people at school that supported me and encouraged me to write this book.

INTRODUCTION:
WHY IS THIS BOOK DIFFERENT?

Success is just the last step of a ladder of failures... (The author)

Is this book really different?:

I've read many programming books in my life. All of them have something in common: They just explain theory and show examples made up by the author. Some of them are inspired and their examples are smart. Some others look completely beyond reality.

I wanted to make a different book, so I started to think in alternative ways to explain the subject.

That's how the main idea of this book came to light.

I am a university professor, so I asked some of my students questions like:

-Imagine a cool programming book. What are you expecting to learn in a utopist book like that?.

The answers may be resumed in these sentences:

Most of them wanted to read something **Easy** and **Understandable.** It seems that the students consider that many of the programming books are too complicated and tedious to learn. They'd love to have something easy to read. This fact seems clear. You don't have to explain something in the difficult way if you want to be understood.

So, the first premise of this book was:

TO MAKE SOMETHING EASY.

The second point they marked is that they wanted to learn things based on real cases, based on facts that are real, that apply to reality.

So, the second premise for the book was:

TO MAKE SOMETHING BASED ON A REAL CASE.

This caused me a problem:

I should have to find a real on-line site, that I could use in order to give examples based on it.

Well, this book is the result and the answer to the previous paragraphs. All the programming sentences will be explained at the same time that the structure and the techniques to build a real-world internet site are shown.

Part I

What do I do? Choosing a subject and designing the site

CHAPTER 1

CHOOSING THE THEMATIC

What do I do?

The first thing you've got to do when you want to program a site is to know exactly the answer to these questions:

- What are we going to do?

- How are we going to do it?

These facts may seem something so obvious that all of the books I've read don't even mention them.

It is supposed that people know what they are doing before they do it... Bad reasoning...

One of the most important lessons that should be extracted from this book is the fact that many programmers don't follow this basic rule.

I've been a programmer and systems analyst (and also a teacher) for more than fifteen years. I've seen the attitudes of many students and low-experienced programmers, and I have one thing in clear: It is absolutely common to find yourself immerse in a project you don't know exactly what it is about, and how it is going to evolve.

Millions of dollars (even billions) have been dilapidated in informatics' projects of all kind just because the programmers started to write the codes before the complete design of the system or the site was made. If these temporary designs change, all the code written in advance becomes worthless.

So, the first and most important rule of this book is this one:

You have to know **Where you go**, and **What you have to do** *BEFORE* any single line of code has been programmed.

It is one thousand times easier to change the design of a site than a programmed source code.

If you start to program "general" things before you've been told exactly the structure of the site, it is a factice proof that the design of the site is inadequate.

What will we do here

In this book we'll develop an educative site.

I expect you'll like this kind of site. I asked my students about the kind of site they would like to read about in a book like this one, and there was no coincidence between them. Everyone suggested a different site. Some of them wanted a browser site. Some others talked about a sports site, some others a news site, etc.

Suddenly, one of them said:

"The page (the page of the course) works alright and all of us use it. I think it will be a good example of a real site"

As this was the only site they all agreed that was a good example, I decided to make the book based on it.

Suppose you are a programmer and that you work in a software company. Your boss comes and tells you:

"We've got a new customer, and I have assigned him to you. You must satisfy his needs. It is Mr. Bosque. He is a university professor that needs an internet site to manage the relationships with his students. The University has an official site, of course, but they allow the professors to have also specific sites for their classes."

Well… from now on, you'll have the task to build an Internet site for a teacher…

Summary:

- You have to know **Where you go**, and **What you have to do** *BEFORE* any single line of code has been programmed.

- It is one thousand times easier to change a design of a site than a programmed source code.

- In this book we'll assume that you are a professional programmer. You will have the task to build an Internet site for me (I am your customer).

CHAPTER 2

WHAT DOES THE CUSTOMER WANT?

What do you want?

In this book we are supposing that you are a professional programmer. That doesn't mean that you are a real programmer in your life (perhaps you are a student, or just a fan of high-tech). However, the attitude that will be taught to you here is the way a professional programmer should behave.

If you are working for a living as a programmer, the customers come to your company and ask for the services of it. The visit becomes in a new project, that is assigned to several analysts or programmers. In old times, it was usual to have vast groups of people for a project:

- A PAO (Personal Account Officer), that was in charge of public relationships. In other words, he was the one who had to speak with the customer. He was the one that had the meetings with the customer.

- A project leader, that was in charge of the work,

- Some systems analysts, that used to make the *"analysis"*

- Programmers, that had to write the source code of it.

Nowadays, we are in an era of flexible employment. It means that you have to make everything (for the same payment). In other words, you have to be a

PAO—leader—analyst—programmer, or at least an analyst—programmer. In this book I will simply use the word "programmer", but I imply any possible combination of the PAO—leader—analyst -programmer work.

When you are working for a customer, it is extremely important to try to know what he wants BEFORE programming anything, because many (or most) of the customers don't know exactly what they want. This is a non-written rule of the programmer.

It is very important for you to remember it. It will save you a lot of time, and many programmer's working hours of your life.

> *Many of the customers don't know exactly what they want*
> *when they ask for your services.*

What happens if I don't follow this rule?

When you have an interview with the customers, they generally tell you vague and ambiguous sentences about their desires.

Words like *"Cool"*, *"on fashion"*, *"vivid colors"*, *"I want something like the ZZZ.com page"*, *"not very postmodern"*, *"just as the style of XXX.com page"* are spoken by the customer during the interviews he has with you.

You start to work based on those sentences, and after many, many hours of your sweat, when you show them what you've done, they just tell you:

-*"Oh, I don't like it, this is not what we talked about… "*

It is in these moments when you start to think about becoming a farmer and use the rest of your life taking care of chickens and pigs.

So, the important lessons to be learnt here are these:

- You have to talk to the customer many times, just to get his feedback.

- Never work too much without showing him what you've done, because he can change his mind and ask you to do again the work.

- Try to "persuade" him to give you as much information as possible about what it means to have a "cool" site, what is his "style" and what is the "image" he wants to project with the site.

Let's go back to our example:

You are the programmer and I am the customer.

Suppose I tell you:

Well, I want a formal site…not so formal that nobody will see it, but not a site with many pictures, buttons and things like that…

One thing you have to realize is that many times the customers start talking about the way they want the site to look like, but they don't tell you what information the site has to exhibit.

So, you know until now that I just want a standard site. I don't want too vivid colors, or animations in it.

That's ok. Not every site needs those things. If you want to make a "serious" site, it is better to do something without too many exuberant add-inns.

The standard structure for a classic site is a page with three frames in it.

The **frames** are hidden windows placed in the pages by the programmers. Look at Table 1 to see this point. When you have a frame structure for a site, in general the one that contains the titles remains fixed, and the inner frame changes every time the user selects an option from the menu.

There are other possible structures for a site, but we would need a book just to talk about all of them, and it is really worthless to do that. It is enough for you just to know that the most popular sites in the Web are designed using a frame structure (and three is the general number of frames they use).

Table 1: Structure of frames in a standard page

FRAME 1 Titles or Horizontal Menu	
FRAME 2: Vertical Menu	FRAME 3: Body of the page

So, at this point you (the programmer) should have to suggest me (the customer) to do a site based on a three-frame design.

If I say "yes", you can go on with the design. In general, the customer does-n't care about the "structure" of the site, so you don't have to worry about it. However, some of them could tell you they like the "XXX.com" site that has another structure. This is the point you have to check now. Many inexpert programmers start to do the site without asking the customers.

Imagine what would happen if you had designed a three-framed site and I tell you: *"Oh, no… That's not what I wanted, the XXX.com site looks better…"*. All your work was worthless.

Summary:

- When you are working for a customer, it is extremely important to try to know what he wants BEFORE programming anything.

- The customer has to confirm the general structure of the site before a single line of code is written.

- Many of the customers don't know exactly what they want when they ask for your services.

- You have to talk to the customer many times, just to get his feedback.

- Never work too much without showing him what you've done, because he can change his mind and ask you to do again the work.

- Try to "persuade" him to give you as much information as possible about what it means to have a "cool" site, what is his "style", what is the "image" he wants to project with the site.

CHAPTER 3

STARTING THE SITE: PRELIMINARY TASKS

How do I start the site?

Now that you know you can make a three-framed structure, we will start talking a bit about programming:

First of all: The site will generally need a domain name (DN). A domain name is that nomenclature that is written like:

http://www.Customername.com

The first characters http://, and www are generally standard. We will not discuss here why you have to type them. Let's focus on the last part of the sentence: Customername.com

If the customer wants a site with his name, the programmer has to register a DN with the name he tells him.

To register a DN is a very simple task: You can do it on-line using the Web.

There are several companies that allow you to do it. Just enter into your favorite browser and use the search menu typing the keywords "register domain name". You will get a list of companies that register domains. It is very easy to do it. You just have to follow the instructions that each page gives you. In general, you first have to check if the domain name is available (you can't use a domain name that has already been registered). If it is free, you just need a valid credit card to do it. Many programmers use their own credit cards, and afterwards they just increase their fees a bit to absorb the cost.

I personally do not consider that this is ethically correct, because this way the owner of the domain name is the programmer, not the customer.

You (the programmer) should ask the customer for a legal credit card and register the domain name using it, so the owner of the name is him.

Many malicious programming companies register the customers' domain names on purpose this way. If the customer wants to fire them and use the services of another programmer, they just "remind" him that they are the legal owners of the domain name, so they try to "sell" it to him. (not at a reasonable prize, of course)

Well… Let's go back to our example:

You are an honest programmer so you ask me (the customer) for my credit card number in order to register my own domain name.

I answer you: *"Oh, no I don't care about a personal domain name."*

The next step is to rent a "hosting" service. (In general, big companies buy their own hosts, so they don't need to rent disk space).The hosting companies are the ones that own the space to place the sites. They rent you a portion of their available space. This service can be found for free in the net, but they place ad banners on the top of the pages.

The programmer should ask the customer if he wants a paid service (no banners) or a free one.

In general big and middle-size companies do not like banners in their sites so they use paid services. However, it is usual to see small business companies and independent professionals that do not want to spend much money in their site, so they prefer the free services.

Well… Suppose you (the programmer) ask me (the customer) about my preferences, and I tell you that as the site has no sponsors nor generates incomes, I'd prefer a free service.

The process to subscribe to a free hosting service is similar as the one we described when we talked about the domain names.

You just have to use your favorite browser, use the search utility, and place the keywords:

"Free Web page hosting "

You'll get a list of sites that offer the service.

In general they give you a username, a password, some megabytes of available space, and a sub-domain name, that is considerable larger than a personal domain name.

An example of sub-domain name could be:

---

http://www.neocity.com/username/

Where http://www.neocity.com is the location of the company that gives you the service and the last "/username" is the name of the customer.

Note: this is not a real site, it was made up just as an example. If you are looking for a REAL hosting company, look in the appendix section, where the source code is placed.

Summary:

Before you start your site you need to have arranged some themes:

- You need to have registered your future domain name, or you have to know that the page will not need a personal DN.

- You need to have some space to place the page.

- You can use the banner-free services of a paid hosting company, or you can use a free service with ads banners.

CHAPTER 4

WHAT DO I PLACE IN THE MAIN PAGE?

Going back to the design of our site:

Perhaps the customer doesn't tell you anything about the way the page must look like, but this is dangerous for the programmer because you have to work first and show him the result, and he may say he doesn't like it, so your work was in vane.

It is easier if the customer has an idea about what he wants. You only have to program something he will probably like, just because he was the one who thought about it. Let's try this alternative here:

Suppose now that I (the customer) tell you (the programmer):

"-Oh, I'd like a main page like this"

and I show you this draft image:

Image 1. Main page

TITLES	Menu	Menu	Menu	Menu Menu
	Logo	**University Name**	**Valid for the**	
			course of:	
		School Name	**Marcelo**	
			Bosque	
Menu		**Subject name**		
Menu		**BACKGROUND**		
		IMAGE HERE		
Menu				
Menu	**Webmaster: You**			

Some aspects to remark:

The site we will discuss here is a real site. I use it to manage the matters of my course at school. As this book has been edited by an American publisher, it cannot be considered an official book of the University, so I prefer to avoid as much as possible any direct mention to its name in it, even though the Internet page does it explicitly. The site is published at:

http://www5.domaindlx.com/mgbosq/index.html.

You can see how it looks like (and get the source code) from there.

I'd like to tell you that this book is edited in black & white only, so we will transform the colors of the real page into a set of gray tones in the images shown here. However, in the real page the background (shown here as a light gray) is beige.

One thing you need to have in mind is that the customers change their minds often. Let's suppose that I do, so some days afterwards I show you a new, renovated version of the page:

In the center of it, now I want an illustration as a background, and some titles placed over it.

I'd like some titles that could say :

"Contents of the course",

"Schedule"

"Student's Files" .

So the page should look like this:

Image 2. Main page

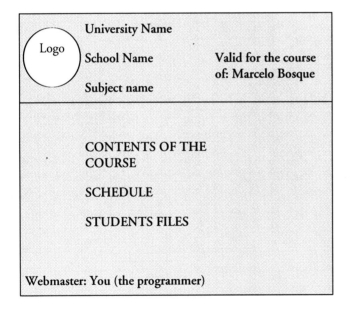

Summary:

- The site we will discuss here is a real site. I use it to manage the matters of my course at school.

- The site is published at:

http://www5.domaindlx.com/mgbosq/index.html.

- You can see how it looks like (and get the source code) from there.

CHAPTER 5

WHEN DO WE START WITH HTML?

As it is said in the previous chapters, you should have a complete perspective of the needs and desires of the customer before you start to write a single line of code, so we should go on talking about the preliminary questions, but I know that many of the readers are impatient and they want to start with the programming. Well...

Let's start seeing some basic aspects of programming.

First of all, you must know that Hypertext Markup Language, best known as HTML is the language you use in Internet pages.

Many popular software packages, as Microsoft WORD, for example, are able to convert their documents into a format that can be published in the net automatically. [1]

A regular user who wants to write a note and to publish it in the net doesn't have to know anything about HTML. WORD does it for them.

However, the professional designer of Internet sites must have the knowledge necessary to program "by hand" in HTML. There are many applications and functions that require a personal retouch of the code, and no automatic code generator can substitute this requirements.

So, remember:

---

[1] Microsoft and Word are trademarks of Microsoft Corp.

The professional designer must know HTML programming. It is not enough to have a software that generates code automatically.

That's why in this book I will not mention any of these code generators.

How do we program a typical HTML file?

HTML works with text files. That means that you can create and modify it using a text editor program, such as WORDPAD or NOTEBOOK , the editors that come with WINDOWS [2]. As I said in the previous chapter, there are software programs that automatically create HTML code, but this code is generally rigid and fixed, so the professional programmer has a lot of problems if he just trusts in them to do the job.

As we were saying, the HTML file is the same as any .txt text file. The only difference is that you have to create a text file and rename it as .htm or .html

---

Summary: All you have to do to create a standard HTML file is to make a text file using any text editor program and rename it (or create it directly) as .htm instead of .txt

---

This will create a file that is ready to be read and published in the net.

---

[2] WINDOWS, WORDPAD and NOTEBOOK are registered trade marks of Microsoft Corporation.

Your First HTML file:

- Open your text editor and create a file first.htm

- Write: HELLO

- Save the file and close it.

The file "first.htm" will be placed in the folder you saved it. Let's suppose it was saved at "My Documents"

Use the Windows Explorer[3] to see the contents of the folder "My Documents".

Find the file first.htm and double-click in it.

Your Internet browser will be opened. Using it you should see a blank page that only says "HELLO".

Congratulations!

This was your first HTML program!.

TIP: HTML understands that any text included in a .htm or .html file is plain text, or just text, so it shows it directly.

As you can see, it is not so difficult to convert a text into a standard HTML file.

However, all that glisters is not gold. It is not so easy to program.

---

[3] Windows Explorer is a registered trade mark of Microsoft Corporation.

There are some conventions and syntactic rules that have to be taken into account when we create HTML files.

First of all:

Every HTML file must start with these characters:

<html>

and must finish with these ones:

</html>

We will call them a TAG. HTML has a lot of tags, that are the specific instructions of the language. All HTML programs must start with the <html> tag and must finish with the </html> tag.

So you should rewrite your first program.

To do it, just open again your text editor and call your file first.htm

When you've got the file in edit mode, you'll see just the "HELLO" word you placed before.

Modify the file, adding the tags.

Your file should look now like:

<html>

HELLO

</html>

Save it and execute it using the same technique shown before. (use the explorer, find the file and double-click with the mouse in it)

Congratulations again!. You've done what we can say a proper HTML page.

Summary:

- The professional designer must know HTML programming. It is not enough to have a software that generates code automatically.

- All you have to do to create a standard HTML file is to make a text file using any text editor program and rename it (or create it directly) as .htm instead of .txt

- HTML understands that any text included in a .htm or .html file is plain text, or just text, so it shows it directly.

- Every HTML file must start with this tag: **<html>** and must finish with this one: **</html>**

CHAPTER 6

NOW THAT I KNOW HTML, HOW DO I SET UP A PAGE?

The HTML files will be executed using the Internet browsers. (Internet Explorer and Navigator are two of the most popular browsers)[4]

These browsers need to know some information about your file to work properly. The HTML files have to provide it to them. We call this process "SETUP" of a standard HTML file.

There are several setup instructions you can place in a file.

Let's see some of them:

Look at this HTML file:

---

[4] Internet Explorer is a trade mark of Microsoft Corp. Netscape Navigator is a trade mark of Netscape corp.

```
<html>

<head>

<meta http-equiv="Content-Language" content="en">

<meta http-equiv="Content-Type" content="text/html;
charset=windows-1252">

<meta name="GENERATOR" content="your editor program">

<meta name="ProgId" content="YourEditor.Document">

<title>My first HTML</title>

</head>

<body>

HELLO

</body>

</html>
```

Here there are several things to notice:

The HTML file has been divided in two sections: The first section starts with the tag <HEAD> and finishes with the tag </HEAD>. The second one starts with the tag <BODY> and finishes with the tag </BODY>

In other words: A typical structure of a standard HTML file is:

```
<html>

        <head>

        </head>

        <body>

        </body>

</html>
```

We will call "Head section" and "Body section" to these divisions of the HTML file.

The head section is used mostly to place the setup instructions of the file, and the body section to write the text of the page.

Usual Setup instructions of the Head Section:

It is usual to place the setup instructions using the **<meta></meta>** tags. These are called Meta-tags.

Let's look at some of them:

<u>**Setting up the language of the page**</u>

```
<meta http-equiv="Content-Language" content="en">
```

This tag tells the browser that the page is written in English.

The final message can be substituted by other combinations as "fr" or "es". For example:

```
<meta http-equiv="Content-Language" content="es">
```

indicates that the page is written in Spanish. As you are an English spoken person, let's always use the first variant.

Telling the browser which set of characters must be used

Every human language has different letters. For example: The stressed letters á, à, é, è, ë, etc. exist in French and Spanish, but not in English.

A set of characters is the combination of valid letters that should have to be used to read and write a message written in the page.

We've already told the browser that the page was written in English. Now we can tell it which character set must it use. The windows-1252 character set is one of the Western Europe international character sets, so it contains most of the letters needed for American English and Western European countries.

Configuring the generator program:

If you want to identify the program you used to create the HTML, you can do it with these two instructions:

```
<meta name="GENERATOR" content="Your Editor program">

<meta name="ProgId" content= "YourEditor.Document">
```

Writing a title for the page

The title of a page is the message that appears when you are browsing in the net and you ask the computer to search something. If a page has no title, nothing appears.

To place a title in a page just use the <title></title> tags in the head section.

```
<title>My first HTML</title>
```

In general, all these setup instructions do not vary from one page to another (only the title varies), so you just can copy them every time you create a new file.

Summary:

- The HTML files will be executed using the Internet browsers.

- The HTML file is divided in two sections: The first section starts with the tag <HEAD> and finishes with the tag </HEAD>. The second one starts with the tag <BODY> and finishes with the tag </BODY>

- It is usual to place the setup instructions using the **<meta></meta>** tags. These are called Meta-tags.

- To place a title in a page just use the <title></title> tags in the head section.

CHAPTER 7

HOW DO I DO TO WRITE TEXT AND INSERT THE IMAGES?

In the previous chapter, we have created a file. We will call it here "main.htm", so this is what we've got until now:

Main.htm – version 1.0

```
<html>
<head>
<meta http-equiv="Content-Language" content="en">
<meta http-equiv="Content-Type" content="text/html; charset=windows-1252">
<meta name="GENERATOR" content="your editor program">
<meta name="ProgId" content="YourEditor.Document">
<title>main.htm</title>
</head>
<body>
</body>
</html>
```

In summary:

- We have placed all the setup commands
- We have created the HTML skeleton

The body section

We have already said that the core section of the page has to be placed inside the <body></body> tags.

Let's concentrate in it now.

Changing the background color

The <body> instruction can setup the background color of the page. In the book you see it gray, but the real color of the page is beige.

The instruction must be written as follows:

<body bgcolor="beige">. What is important for you to know now is that you can write the name of the common colors as:

<body bgcolor="yellow">

If you want to place an image (instead of a color) as background, you can use the clause "*background*":

Example: <body background="xx.gif">

where xx.gif is the image you want to place as background.

Next, we have to start placing the text and the images.

Working with paragraphs

The tags <p></p> are used to identify paragraphs.

Look at this example:

```
<p>Hello</p><p>Everybody</p>
```

When you see it using the internet browser, it will appear like this:

```
Hello

Everybody
```

A paragraph can also be aligned, using the ALIGN clause:

You can select the alignment of the text using the commands:

align="right", align="left" and align="center".

Example:

```
<font size="1" face="Arial" align="center" >Hello Everybody</font>
```

The page will be seen like this:

```
                            Hello Everybody
```

Look at this example:

```
<p align="center"> Hello </p> <p align="left"> Everybody </p>
```

This will be seen like this:

Hello
Everybody

How to give format to a text:

Texts can be placed in **BOLD** using the <b></b> tags, or in *italics* using the <i></i> ones. You can use it alone , or in the middle of a paragraph (between <p></p>)

Example:

```
<p> <b>Hello </b> </p> <p align= "left"> <I>Everybody</I> </p>
```

This will be seen like this:

Hello
Everybody

If you want to setup the font and size of the text, we can use the tags <font></font> to do it.

Example:

```
<font size="1" face="Arial">Hello Everybody</font>
```

The page will be seen like this:

Hello Everybody

This text is written using ARIAL font and size=1.

If you work with WORD [5] or any other word processor, perhaps this could seem confusing to you. WORD works with fonts that are shown in terms of their respective DPI (dots per inch). So, we use to think in terms of 10,12,14 DPIs when we want to setup the size of a font.

HTML works different. It only has seven predefined sizes, so you just can choose between one of them.

If you want to know what they mean, see the following table:

Font Sizes

HTML	WORD
1	8
2	10
3 / Normal	12
4	14
5	18
6	24
7	36

You can also combine the <font></font> instructions with the paragraph markers. The final sentence could look like this:

---

[5] WORD, and Microsoft WORD are trademarks of Microsoft Corp.

```
<p align="left"><b>

<font size="1" face="Arial">Hello Everybody</font>

</b></p>
```

Inserting images:

Images are located in .gif, .jpg, .tif or .bmp files.

All of these graphic formats are supported automatically.

Suppose you've got this image:

The image is stored in a file called logo.gif

We can use the instruction <img> to insert it in the page.

Let's see an example:

```
<img border="0" src="logo.gif" width="100" height="105">
```

The clause BORDER="0" means that the image will be shown as it is, without a border. BORDER="1" adds a border to it.

The clause scr="logo.gif" makes reference to the file that contains the image. In our case it is called "logo.gif".

You can also setup the size of the file with the optional clauses WIDTH and HEIGHT. If you don't use them, the file is shown in its real size. If you place a value here, the browser understands that it is a DPI (dots per inch) value, so the image is expanded or decreased until it reaches these width and height values.

In the last example, width="100" and height="150". The image has to be resized into a 100 x 150 dpi display size.

Using tables

When you have text and images in a page, it is easier to work if you make a table with rows and columns, and you place the elements in different cells of it.

You can create a table using the tags:

<table></table>

The table can be configured to show its borders or not.

This example creates a table without visible borders that uses 100% of the width of the page

```
<table border="0" width="100%">
```

The next example creates a table with visible borders that uses 50% of the width of the page

```
<table border="1" width="50%">
```

Our page looks like this now

Main.htm – version 1.1

```
<html>
<head>
<meta http-equiv="Content-Language" content="en">
<meta http-equiv="Content-Type" content="text/html; charset=windows-1252">
<meta name="GENERATOR" content="your editor program">
<meta name="ProgId" content="YourEditor.Document">
<title>main.htm</title>
</head>
<body bgcolor="beige">
<table border="1" width="50%">
</table>
</body>
</html>
```

As a matter of fact, the instruction <table></table> only tells the browser that a table will be included in that part of the page. No more.

Now, we have to declare the number of rows and columns contained in the table.

We've got two orders to do that:

<tr></tr> for rows and <td></td> for columns in a row (you may also think about them as "cells in a row").

Suppose this structure:

<table border="1" width="100%">

<tr>

<td></td><td></td><td></td>

</tr>

</table>

You are creating a table with one row and three columns (or cells) in it. It will look like this:

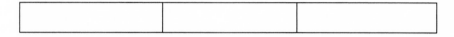

Notice that we have to define the ROWS first, and then place the columns INSIDE the rows, or in other words, the <td></td> instructions must be inside the <tr></tr> tags.

To place text or images in a cell we just have to write the sentences between the tags.

Example:

```
<table border="1" width="100%">

<tr>

<td>A</td><td>B</td><td>C</td>

</tr>

</table>
```

The table will look like this:

A	B	C

If we want the text centered, we can use the instruction ALIGN in the tags:

Let's write now:

```
<table border="1" width="100%" >
<tr><td align="center">A</td><td>B</td><td>C</td></tr>
</table>
```

Now, the table will look like this:

A	B	C

You may also want to setup a different size for each column:

If you make the borders invisible using BORDER="0", it will look like this:

A   B   C

As a matter of fact, this is the structure we'll use in the page, because it is the easiest way to place text and images in a page in different locations.

Working this way is like doing it with a spread sheet program. You just place the text in the cells and the table aligns them for you.

Writing comments

A comment is a "note". You can place them in the source code to remind you what the code means. It will not appear in the page.

You just have to write the text inside the "<! >" tags.

Example:

<! This is a comment. I want to see it in the source code, but I don't want to see it in the published page >

How to place a hyperlink:

Just use the <a href></a> tags.

Examples:

<a href="http://www.moma.org>Visit Moma site </a>

<a href="http://www.moma.org" target="mainframe">Visit Moma site </a>

The page looks like this:

Visit Moma site

When you click on the sentence, the site http://www.moma.org will be loaded. If you have a frame structure as the main structure of your site, you will also need to use the sentence "target". In this case , the site will only be loaded in that specific frame. If you omit it, the page will be loaded using the full screen.

Summary:

- The core section of the page has to be placed inside the <body></body> tags.

- The <body> instruction can be used to setup the background color of the page.

- If you want to place an image instead of a color as background, you can use the clause "*background*", *as in* <body background="xx.gif">.

- A paragraph can also be aligned, using the ALIGN clause:

- You can place a comment in the source code to remind you what the code means. It will not appear in the page. Use the "<! >" tags.

- The <a href></a> tags are used to write a hyperlink .

Chapter 8

Suppose I want to change ALL the fonts of the site at the same time... Could I make it?

One of the problems of the professional programmer, is that the aspect of the pages must be changed from time to time. Users get bored easily. They want to see some changes in the page to feel that it is still "cool". In general, they just pay attention to the external part of it, the way it looks like, so you have to change the covers (main pages) to cause this effect. The problem is that if we want to make global format changes in the page we will spend a lot of time. Just think that every <FONT>, <P>, and <A> clauses should be changed in all the pages that are part of the site.

As you may imagine, this would be an extremely big effort, and it would consume many labor hours to make it.

In order to find a better solution, some setup files were created. They were called Cascade Style Sheets Files or CSS. They are separate text files (from the HTMLs), and they use the .CSS extension. You can also create them with any text editor.

What is a CSS file for?:

Very simple: you can place there the setup configuration of the clauses once , so all of them will follow these instructions.

For example, you can write there that each time you write a <FONT> clause, you mean you want it written in "Arial" font, size=1 (8 dpi), bold and italic. Every <FONT> clause in the page will follow this command automatically.

Now suppose that you want to change the fonts of all the site at once. All you have to do is to change the <FONT> clause setup in the CSS file, and VOILA!: All the site is changed.

You can do the same with the background colors, so you can periodically change the colors of your page with a minimum effort. The users will feel that the page was renewed, at an insignificant cost.

As you may imagine, the CSS files are extremely powerful tasks that save hundreds of working hours to the programmers.

So, in this chapter, we will have to talk about them a bit.

Creating a CSS file

So, open your favorite text editor. Make a new file. Call it "styles.css". (In the real site, this file is called "estilos.css")

Write this line and save the file:

```
P {font-family: Verdana, Arial, Helvetica}
```

What does it mean?

P is the HTML clause <P></P>.

The CSS file is telling the page that every time you place a <P></P> clause, you want the text in it written in "Verdana" font. If this font is not installed in the user's computer, then the page must write it using "Arial" font. If none of them are installed, then you want it written in "Helvetica".

Now look at this:

```
P          {font-family: Verdana, Arial, Helvetica}
A          {color:#D3D3D3}
A:hover    {COLOR:lightgreen }
```

Here you are adding instructions for the behavior of the **<A href=></A>** clauses. Remember they are used to place a hyperlink.

The links at the <A> clause will be shown in #D3D3D3 color that is a green tone. You don't need to know the "#" configuration codes. However, let me tell you that you have three methods to place a color definition:

a) The RGB (Red, Green, Blue) method, where you setup a color as **color= RGB(102,102,153).** The numbers imply the strength of red, green and blue in a scale from 0 to 255.

b) The # method, where you place the RGB colors using Hexadecimal code, so they may vary from 0 to FF (**color=#000000 to color=#FFFFFF)**

c) The easiest method (the one I recommend you to use): You can just place the name of the color as : color="yellow".

This is the method used in **A:hover** that is the event when the mouse is placed over the link.

In other words: You are telling the computer you want ALL the links of the page in a green tone, and when the user places the mouse over it you want the color to change to a light green tone.

I expect that these few examples could be enough to show you how easy it is to change the global setup of the page using a CSS file.

Creating classes

A class is a configuration that can be applied to any clause you want.

They are identified with the use of the dot (.).

Example

```
.Title2 {color:black ; font-family: Monotype Corsiva; Arial,
Helvetica;font-size: 14pt; line-height: 12pt; font-weight:bold;text-align:
center }
```

Here we've just defined a class called .Title2 that orders the computer to place a text in black, with a font "Monotype Corsiva" (or Arial and Helvetica if it is not installed), with a 12pt size (look that here we use the dpi code , the same way you use it in WORD[6]), in bold weight, and with centered alignment.

So, every clause that uses the class **.Title2**, will be shown using these characteristics.

Example:

```
<p class=Title2>Hello</p>
```

This will show any text between <p> and </p> like this:

```
                              Hello
```

---

[6] WORD is a trademark of Microsoft Corp.

You can use a class with any HTML clause, so if you write:

```
<font class=Title2>Hello</font>
```

you will get the same effect, because you are telling the clause <Font> that it must be setup with the directions given by class=title2

Note the difference between these statements:

- **P {color: Arial}**:This affects all <p> statements

- **<p class=Title2>**:This affects just the <p> statements that uses the class=title2 option included. All the other <p> clauses are not changed.

In other words: CSS files allow you two types of configuration:

A really global one, where you setup the clause itself as:

- P {color: Arial}

A partial global one that affects only the clauses that have the "**class=**" option included.

How to enable the CSS file:

If you want to use a CSS file, and you want it to be recognized by the HTML file, you need to "call" it from the code:

In the middle of the <HEAD></HEAD> section of the HTML (the Standard Head Section) you have to place this order:

```
<STYLE type=text/css>@import URL("styles.css");</STYLE>
```

You have to change "styles.css" for the name of your CSS file. This sentence has to be installed in all HTML files, so it is a good idea to include it as part of the Standard head section of every file.

A complete CSS setup file is included in the Appendix section of this book. The real CSS file can be downloaded from the site.

CHAPTER 9

CAN I MAKE THE MAIN PAGE NOW?

This chapter starts with a question: Can I make the main page now?

The answer is YES, and NO, at the same time.

In the first chapters, we have said we were going to use a three-framed structure for our main page. We also said that a frame is an internal window of the page that is invisible to the user.

You don't know how to make it yet. However, the third frame (the central frame) is where we must place the page that the customer told us to design.

So, in this chapter we will make the third frame of the main page, and in the next chapters we'll see how to concatenate it with the other frames.

Let's remember that I (in my role of customer) had asked you (in your role of programmer) to design this:

Image 3. Main page- Inner frame

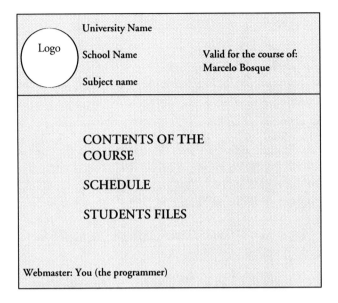

So you (the programmer) start to write the page, using the elements you've got. You decide to call the page "main.htm"

After a few hours, you end the code:

Let's look at it closer:

```
<table border="0" width="100%"> <! YOU CREATE A TABLE>

<tr> <! YOU CREATE THE FIRST ROW>

<td ><img border="0" src="logo.gif' width="100" height="105"></td> <!
YOU CREATE THE FIRST COLUMN OF THAT ROW, AND YOU
PLACE THERE THE IMAGE THAT CONTAINS THE LOGO>

<td ><p align="left"><b><font size="1" face="Arial">University name
</font></b></p> <! YOU CREATE THE SECOND COLUMN OF
THAT ROW, AND YOU WRITE THE UNIVERSITY NAME
THERE, IN BOLD ; ARIAL FONT, SIZE 1 >

<p align="left"><b><font size="1" face="Arial">School Name</font>
</b></p> <! YOU WRITE THE SCHOOL NAME >

<p align="left"><b><font size="1" face="Arial">Subject Name</font>
</b></p> <! YOU WRITE THE SUBJECT NAME >

</td><! YOU CLOSE THE COLUMN >

<td ><! YOU OPEN NEXT COLUMN OF THE SAME ROW>

<p align="left"><b><font size="1" face="Arial">Valid for the course of:
</font></b></p>

 <p align="left"><b><font size="1" face="Arial">Marcelo Bosque</font>
</b></p><! YOU WRITE THE TEXT THERE>

</td><! YOU CLOSE THE COLUMN>

 </tr><! YOU CLOSE THE ROW>

</table><! YOU CLOSE THE TABLE>
```

So, until now, you have done this part of the page:

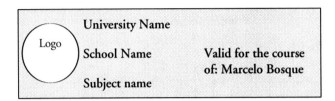

Let's program now the second part of the page: (Remember we've got an image as a background and the text over it)

> **CONTENTS OF THE COURSE**
>
> **SCHEDULE**
>
> **STUDENTS RECORDS**
>
> Webmaster: You (the programmer)

```
<! At this point you have done the fist part of the page>

<table border="0" width="100%" align=center><! OPEN A TABLE>

<tr><! OPEN A ROW>

<td width="75%" background="fce.jpg" height="250"><! OPEN A
COLUMN IN ROW1 AND PLACE THE IMAGE FCE.JPG AS
BACKGROUND>

<p align="center"><b><font color="blue" size="6"> Contents of the
course</font></b></p><! WRITE TEXT. NOTE THAT WE USE
SIZE=6 (BIG SIZE)>

<p align="left"><b><font color="blue" size="5"> Schedule </font></b>
</p><! WRITE TEXT>

<p align="left"><b><font color="blue" size="5"> Students Records</font>
</b></p><! WRITE TEXT>

</td></tr></table><! CLOSE COLUMN, ROW AND TABLE. NOTE
THAT YOU CAN DO IT IN A SINGLE CODE LINE>

<p align="left"><font size="2">Webmaster: (You)</font></p>
```

Congratulations!:

At this point, you should be able to program the main.htm file, that is your first real html page.

You've got the source code in the Appendix Section. You can download the source code from http://www5.domaindlx.com/mgbosq/main.htm.

Chapter 10

Tell me how to go on with the main page of the site

In the previous chapter we have seen how to program one of the frames of the main page.

Our structure should be then:

FRAME 1 Titles or Horizontal Menu	
FRAME 2: Vertical Menu	Frame 3: Body of the page (main.htm)

Each frame must be written in a different file, so we'll need three files, one for each frame. However, we will need an extra file to work as the initial page. It will only be a kind of router, a page that redirects and sends the user to each specific frame. In other words: The three-framed structure consists in four files. Let's see how to write this fourth file.

Designing the initial file

Create a file called "index.html". The first part of it (the head section) should be familiar to you now, so I'll just write it down. Look at it and if you don't understand it, go back to the previous chapters.

```
<HTML>

<HEAD>

<TITLE>index. html</TITLE>

<META http-equiv=Content-Type content="text/html; charset=windows-1252">

<META content="youreditor" name=GENERATOR>

</HEAD>
```

Let's see now how to define the environment to work with frames:

First of all, we have to define what is called a FRAMESET, that is the skeleton where the frames are supported.

We can use the instruction FRAMESET

Look at the following table:

```
<FRAMESET border=false frameSpacing=0 rows=100,* frameBorder=0>
```

Here we have defined a frameset with an invisible external border (border=false) and also with no inner borders between the frames (frameborder=0), with no blank space between the frames (framespacing=0), and 100 rows of length.

The frameset is just the skeleton. Once you have created it, you have to setup the three inner frames that constitute the main page.

Designing Frame 1

DOING NOW: FRAME 1 Titles or Horizontal Menu	
TO DO!	TO DO!

To set up each frame we have to use the tag FRAME.

Look at the following table:

```
<FRAME name=top marginWidth=0 marginHeight=0 src="menuhori.
htm" scrolling=no >
```

The instructions MarginWidth and MarginWeight configure the width and weight of the margins, and the scrolling command allows the user to scroll or not with the mouse in the frame. The other options are:

Name=top. We assign a name to the frame. In this case we have called it "top"

Scr= The name of a standard html file. Here we are telling the browser the name of the file that must be placed in the window (the frame). In other words: We are telling the browser that we will create a file called "menuhori.htm" that will contain frame 1.

Designing Frame 2

FRAME 1 DONE!	
DOING NOW: FRAME 2 Vertical Menu	TO DO!

First of all we define the FRAMESET for frame 2

```
<FRAMESET cols=173,*>
```

Then we define the FRAME for frame 2

```
<FRAME name=menu marginWidth=0 marginHeight=0
src="menuvertical.htm" scrolling=yes
target="mainframe"></FRAMESET>
```

As you see, we have named it "menu" in the instruction:

name=menu

and it loads a file called menuvertical.htm . This is said in the instruction:

scr="menuvertical.htm"

It means that we will have to create a file "menuvertical.htm" that will contain the frame 2.

The most important frame is frame 3. We will create it now.

Designing Frame 3

DONE!	
DONE!	DOING NOW: FRAME 3 Main.htm

We can just configure the name and scr.

```
<FRAME name=mainframe scr="main.htm">
```

The browsers can be setup in such a way that they do not allow to show pages with frames. The following command is only activated if this circumstance happens and shows a message warning the user about this fact.

```
<NOFRAMES>
<p>This page uses frames, but your explorer does not allow them.</p>
</NOFRAMES></FRAMESET></HTML>
```

Summary of the chapter:

The main page will be called "index.html" and contains the skeleton of a three-framed structure.

Each frame will load a different HTML file.

Frame 1 (the titles frame) will show menuhori.htm

Frame 2 (the menu frame) will show menuvertical.htm

Frame 3 (the central frame) will display main.htm , that is the file you created in the previous two chapters. So, our structure is:

Main Page: (index.html)

Frame 1 (menuhori.htm)	
Frame 2	Frame 3
(menuvertical.htm)	Main.htm

You've got the source code of the files in the Appendix Section. You can download the source code from:

http://www5.domaindlx.com/mgbosq/index.html.

CHAPTER 11

NOW THAT I'VE DONE THE INNER PART OF MY MAIN PAGE, I NEED A MENU. HOW DO I DO IT?

In the first chapters you've been warned that the programmer needs to have a fluid dialog with the customer and know exactly was he wants BEFORE programming the page, because he might change his mind.

In the last chapters we've been discussing some facts about programming, but this was made just because I suppose the readers (that means you) are eager to see the HTML code and I didn't want to bother you talking too much about the preliminary tasks. However, now has come the time where we have to go back to the dialog programmer-customer.

You (the programmer) have to know what I (the customer) want in order to make a menu.

Suppose we have some work meetings. During them I keep on telling you what I expect to include in the site.

The following table contains a summary of the requests I've told you.

REQUESTS OF THE SITE GIVEN BY THE CUSTOMER
The Customer wants:
A page with the schedule for next quarter period.
Some place to publish all the articles, comments, monographs, and other written works made by the professor and his assistants. It could be named "Publications from the course"
Some place dedicated to the students. They must be able to fill on-line the course admission forms required by the school and the course.
A page that could contain all the research works made by the students
Note: All of this items could be placed in the vertical menu at FRAME 2. The horizontal menu of FRAME 1, could contain links to:
An "about us" page, where the assistants and the professor could introduce their resumes and academic curricula.
The Magisterial guide, that is a guide published by the school with "cases" for the students.[7]

---

[7] A case is the description of a situation that happened into a corporation, bureau or institution, and is used to train the students. The UBA magisterial guide of cases for Information Technology exists in the real world in the original Spanish version, and it can be obtained at school , because the royalties belong to the university. By the way, it was written by the titular (the chief) of the Information Technology Department and me.

| The guide of exercises of the course. Part I (theory). |
| The guide of exercises of the course. Part II (practice). |
| A table of Contents of the subject. |
| The academic rules valid for the course. |
| A survey for the students. |

Well, suppose this is the information you've got until now.

Of course, we have to create one o more pages for each of these themes. However, now we will focus on the menu. The main page must contain a menu with hyperlinks to these future pages.

The first thing you have to do to make a menu is to create a new html page with a Standard Head Section (SHS). We will call this page menu-vertical.htm

Look at the following example:

Menuvertical.htm- Standard Head Section

```
<HTML>
<HEAD>
<TITLE>menuvertical.htm</TITLE>
<META http-equiv=Content-Type content="text/html; charset=iso-8859-1">
<STYLE type=text/css>@import URL("estilos.css");</STYLE>
<META content="youreditor" name=GENERATOR>
<META content="Marcelo Bosque" name=AUTHOR>
</HEAD>
```

You can see here another <Meta> tag that is the

```
<META content="Marcelo Bosque" name=AUTHOR>
```

sentence. It is optional and gives you the opportunity to place your name in the program as the author of it.

The other new sentence is:

```
<STYLE type=text/css>@import URL("estilos.css");</STYLE>
```

The <STYLE></STYLE> tag is also optional and calls a style file. We've already seen style files in a previous chapter.

Once we've got a Standard Head Section (SHS), we have to program the menu itself.

In order to do it, we need to write the <BODY> </BODY> section of the program:

We just have to create a table , with several rows and only one column. Each cell of the table will have a hyperlink to the option desired.

Important: All links must have the TARGET clause in them.

Some of them are pointed to "mainframe" that is the name of FRAME 3.

```
<a href=xx.xx TARGET=mainframe>XX</a>
```

These links will call a page, that will be loaded in the central frame. This fact gives the feeling of a page that changes its inner part but lets the menus fixed every time you click on them.

There is a link that points to "menu". Menu is the name of the second FRAME, in other words, the frame where the vertical menus are placed.

```
<a target="menu" href="menuvertalu.htm"> Students </a>
```

This menu then, is calling another menu that will be placed over it. This gives the user the feeling that a menu is replaced by another menu.

As we saw in the previous chapters, orders like <FONT></FONT> are used, so the standard structure for a link will be something like this:

```
<tr> *** Creates a row

<td> *** Creates the cell (The column for that row)

<FONT> *** Setups the font for that cell

<a href=xx.xx target=mainframe>XX</a> *** makes the link

</FONT></td></tr> *** Closes row, cell and font
```

The links are placed in the BODY section of the program:

```
<BODY >

<TABLE border=1>

<tr><TD height=14 align="center"><FONT><a target="_top" href="indexit.html"> Home </a></FONT></TD></tr>

<tr><TD height=14 align="center"><FONT><a target="mainframe" href="crono2003.htm"> Schedule</a></FONT></TD></tr>
```

```
<tr><TD height=14 align="center"><FONT><A target=_top href="in-
dexpublish.html"> Publications of the course</A></FONT> </TD></tr>

<tr><TD height=14 align="center"><FONT><a target="menu" href=
"menuvertalu.htm"> Students </a> </FONT></TD></tr>

<tr> <TD height=14 align="center"><FONT><A target= mainframe
href="trabajoinv.htm">Student's Research Works</A></FONT></TD>
</tr>

</TABLE>

</BODY>
```

The complete source code for menuvertical.htm is in the Appendix Section or you can download it from http://www5.domaindlx.com/ mgbosq/menuvertical.htm.

So: at this point of the work we've got:

Main Page: (index.html) *DONE!*

Frame 1 (menuhori.htm) *TO DO NOW!*	
DONE! Frame 2 menuvertical.htm_	*DONE!* Frame 3 Main.htm

All that is left now is the code of FRAME 1.

The top rows of any page can be used in two standard ways:

a) To show titles or banners.

b) As a menu. The horizontal menu is the other option that we've got to direct the user to the different options of the site.

In the page, we are going to do a little bit of both:

Now, we'll see how to do the "menuhori.htm" file.

First of all, we need a STANDARD HEAD SECTION (SHS) for the file.

This is the last time a head section will be placed for you to see. They are all the same. One important thing for you to remember, is that the good programmer tries to reuse as much code as he can, because this saves a lot of time to his work, and the professional programmer is always pressed by his boss in order to finish the pages as quickly as he can.

So remind one of the golden rules of the programmer:

GOLDEN RULE I OF THE PROGRAMMER:

REUSE THE CODES AS MUCH AS POSSIBLE.

Save your time. Time is money and time is efficiency.

Standard Head Section of a HTML file

```
<HTML><HEAD><TITLE>menuhori</TITLE>

<META http-equiv=Content-Type content="text/html; charset=iso-8859-1">

<STYLE type=text/css>@import URL("estilos.css");</STYLE>

<META content="youreditor" name=GENERATOR>

<META content="Marcellux" name=AUTHOR>

</HEAD>
```

From now on, we will just refer as the STANDARD HEAD SECTION (SHS), but we won't make emphasis in it anymore.

The <BODY></BODY> Section will just have a table, with one single row and many cells (columns) in it, so the basic skeleton will be something like:

```
<TABLE>

<TR><td></td><td></td><td></td></TR>

</TABLE>
```

The first cell will have an image inserted in it, so we'll have to use a <img> tag.

The second cell will have a title, so we'll place the <FONT></FONT> command in it.

The other cells will be menus, so they just will contain <a href> orders inside.

The skeleton will look like this:

```
<TABLE><TR>
<td><img></td>
<td><a href></td>
<td><a href></td>
</TR></TABLE>
```

Let's look at the real code now:

```
<BODY >

<TABLE>

<TR><TD><img border="0" src= "logofacu-ch.gif" ></TD>

<TD height=21><p align="center"><b><font size="1" face="Arial" color=
"#800000">Subject Name</font></b></p></TD>

<TD><FONT><a target="mainframe" href="nosotros.htm"> About us</a>
</FONT></TD>

<TD><FONT><a target="mainframe" href="GUIDE">Exercises Guide</a>
</FONT></TD>

<TD><FONT><a target="menu" href="menuteo.htm">Exercises for Theory</a>
</FONT></TD>

<TD><font><a target="mainframe" href="Exercises.htm"> Exercises with solu-
tions included</a></font></TD>

<TD ><FONT><a target="_top" href="http://www.econ.uba.ar/www/departa-
mentos/sistemas/plan97/tecn_informac/seoane/seoane/index.htm">    Academic
Rules</a></FONT></TD>

<TD ><FONT><a target="mainframe" href="program.htm"> Subject Curri-
cula</a></FONT></TD>

<TD> <FONT><a target="mainframe" href="survey.htm"> Survey </a>
</FONT> </TD>

</TR></TABLE><BR></BODY></HTML>
```

Once we've done the menu, the question is now:

How do we create a text file to place information in it?

Creating a standard file to place information

We've already seen all the elements needed to do it.

Suppose we want to have a form in the page where the students could send their names and all the personal data required by the course. The instructions could be placed in a page like this:

Example of a file with information: (The following table is an example, not part of the text of the book)

How to fill the form
… After you have filled the form, you have to send it pressing the button that is located at the end of the page. This will add your personal data to the internal database of the course…

To do a page like this is very simple. All you need is:

a)	The Standard Head Section (SHS)
b)	A Table
c)	The text inside the table

We will call this structure a **STANDARD TEXT FILE (STF)** , that can be seen as the common way we will use to place text and images in each page of the site that requires it.

As we have already seen those elements, we'll write the code directly.

```
<HTML><HEAD>
<META http-equiv=Content-Type content="text/html; charset=windows-
1252">
<META content="youreditor" name=GENERATOR>
<STYLE type=text/css>@import URL("estilos.css");</STYLE>
</HEAD><BODY>

<TABLE> <TR> <TD>How to fill the form</TD></TR>
 <TR><TD>
   Alter you  have filled the form, you have to send it pressing the button
that is located at the end of the page. This will add your personal data to
the internal database of the course.
</TD></TR></TABLE></BODY></HTML>
```

Part II

A small step for the customer, a big leap for the programmer

Chapter 12

Nothing is as easy as it seems

If you were able to reach this part of the book, it seems that you have (at least) understood something of the procedure to create a page in HTML.

From the point of view of the customer, what you have to do now is very easy: Just do the site.

From the point of view of the programmer, the task is monumental: He has to program the whole site.

It has been said that the professional programmer has to optimize his time. He is not only paid to do his job, but to do it as soon as possible. To finish the work on time is as important as the work itself.

The low-experienced programmer is always trying to do his best, to create something cool. There's nothing wrong with this at the first sight.

However, it is absolutely usual the fact that he looses the perspective of time while he does it. It means that if the customer said he wanted (or he needed) the work for last Monday, the work HAD TO BE DONE on Monday.

The programmer may say that he is doing the coolest page of the world, and that takes time, so that's the reason why it is not ready, bla, bla, bla...

This part of the book is called *"A small step for the customer"*.

This means that for him, everything is easy: He said he wanted the work for last Monday, so he was expecting to have it last Monday. Your explanations sound to his ears like excuses given by incompetent people to justify their failures. Sometimes it is not the customer the one who establishes the schedule but your boss. It doesn't matter who it is. If someone made an agreement with the customer saying the work should be ready in a specific day, the work has to be ready that day.

The programmer may think he is a kind of "creative genius" , and that geniuses need time to create. My friend: let me tell you something I've learnt after more than fifteen years of practice in the art of programming:

"No matter what you think of yourself, or how good you believe you are. In order to show your boss and the customer that you are an efficient programmer you have to deliver your work in time".

In Part I of the book, we've seen the Golden Rule I of the programmer: *"Reuse your code as much as possible".*

There is a popular phrase that says "Do no reinvent the wheel", meaning that if some problem was already solved, it is nonsense to start again to think about it. We have to use our time and creativity to look for new answers, to ask new questions.

If there are repetitive tasks to program in your site (and every site has a lot of them), you should perform a program the first time to do it, and then you should use this model as a standard way to solve the other similar events that the site has.

Let's look at what we've got until now:

a) Each page has a Head Section. We've made a **STANDARD HEAD SECTION (SHS)** for the pages, so we just should copy it in each new page. We shouldn't have to design a new one.

b) Most of the HTML pages of the site show information. We've made a **STANDARD TEXT FILE (STF)** just to show information. It is the instru.htm page that is shown in FRAME 3. Each time we need to place data in the site we can use this structure.

c) Many pages are modules of the site. A standard module is a set of one or more html files that are used for a specific task. We have created a three framed module that consists in a menu structure that is used to place in the central frame the options selected. It consists in four files:

> Index.html: Contains the skeleton of the frames.

> Menuhori.htm: It uses FRAME1 and displays a menu in horizontal way.

> Menuvertical.htm: It uses FRAME2 and displays a menu in vertical way.

> Main.htm: It uses FRAME3 (the central part of the page)

We will call this structure a **STANDARD MENU MODULE (SMM)**. Each time that we need to create a part of the site where a sub menu appears and displays pages in the inner frame, we will use this module.

STRUCTURE OF THE SITE:

If we use the elements that we've just learnt, we can deduct that the standard structure of a site can be displayed this way:

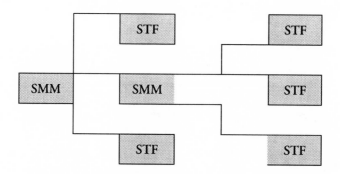

What does it mean?

We have already said that we were going to use a three framed structure for the main page of the site. Later on, we saw we were going to use a menu structure in frames 1 and 2. The Standard Menu Module can be applied to this situation, so we'll use it here. The menus of the SMM can be linked to

a) A serial of files, each one containing an option required by the customer

b) Another menu, (or submenu), that can be represented using the Standard Menu Module or SMM. This menu directs the user to a serial of SFTs.

In summary: The site is a Web (or a net) of SMMs that end in TSFs.

Let's remember what I wanted:

REQUESTS OF THE SITE GIVEN BY THE CUSTOMER The Customer wants:	STANDARD STRUCTURE THAT CAN BE USED
A page with the schedule for next quarter period.	SFT
Some place to publish all the articles, comments, monographs, and other written works made by the professor and his assistants. It could be named "Publications from the course"	As there are many publications we should need another menu (or a submenu) that could links us the each work. A **SMM** could be useful here.
Some place dedicated to the students, where they may be able to fill on-line the course admission forms required by the university and the course.	If there is only one form, we could use a STF. As there are many forms to download we should need another menu structure. Another **SMM** could be useful here.
A page that could contain all research works made by the students	IDEM. (The same as above) SMM
Note: All of these items could be placed in the vertical menu at FRAME 2. The horizontal menu of FRAME 1, should contain links to:	
An "about us" page, where the assistants and the professor could introduce their resumes and academic curricula.	STF

The Magisterial guide, that is a guide published by the school with "cases" for the students. (A case is the description of a situation that happened into a corporation, bureau or institution that is used to train the students).	STF
The guide of exercises of the course. Part I (theory).	SMM
The guide of exercises of the course. Part II (practice).	SMM
Table of Contents of the subject.	STF
Academic Rules valid for the course.	STF
A survey for the students.	STF

All of the STF structures are just text files that have the same structure as the source code given in instru.htm. There is no need to show them again. Just use the STF structure and write in them the appropriate text. In the published page at http://www5.domaindlx.com/mgbosq/index.html you can find the source code of all of them if you need it.

All the SMM structures are the files that are used in those cases where you need to have a menu (horizontal or vertical) that could link you to a serial of specific options of your site.

It is the same skeleton as the source files shown in the book (index.html, menuhori.htm, menuvertical.htm, main.htm), so we don't need to write them again. Just use this structure and change the menus with your new options.

Download the files from the page if you need them.

Part III

Time for ASP

Chapter 13

Asp, Asp, What's that?

Introduction to Asp

Asp means "Active Server Pages", and it is used to work with databases. When you want to store and retrieve data from one of them, we need to work with it. It is used as a complement of HTML.

The principal difference is that it is a language that is executed in the servers, not in the client.

We call a "server" to the computer where your page is published. The client is the machine of the user who is looking at it.

What does it mean?. Very simple: The ASP program runs first and then shows the results to the user. In HTML you can see the source code of all the page whenever you want. In ASP you just see a page generated by the language. That means that you can not see the source code of a complete ASP page. You just see what the programmer lets you see.

In order to work with ASP, we need an ASP server that is a computer that was setup to work with it. Not all servers allow ASP access to them. You have to ask if the server where you want to publish your page allows ASP programming before choosing it.

What is a database?

It is the way we use to store data in the server.

We can think about it as a group of TABLES, related the ones with the others. (Do not confuse this table with the <TABLE></TABLE> HTML command. It has nothing to do. Here the word table is used meaning a group of rows (or columns) related the ones with the others. If we use the specific vocabulary of databases, the rows are called "records", and the columns are called "fields".

So, when we place together a group of related fields, we have a table. A group of tables is a database.

Why do we need ASP in our page?

Let's go back to our site. Remember it? You were the programmer and I was the customer. You are designing my site…

Well… At this point of the book we have to suppose that you've done all the HTML part of the site. The skeleton is ready, the frames have already been created, all the menus have been done, and all the plain text has been added to the site. The CSS files have been created, so you can manage the setup of the page at your will.

Let's suppose that you have already shown me your improvements, and that I liked them.

It is time to go on working…

You had a table with my requests. Many of them were Standard Text Files, and Standard Menu Modules, so we suppose you already did them.

So, look at what we've got now:

REQUESTS OF THE SITE GIVEN BY THE CUSTOMER The Customer wants:	STANDARD STRUCTURE THAT CAN BE USED
Some place dedicated to the students, where they may be able to fill on-line the course admission forms required by the university and the course.	If there is only one form, we could use a STF. As there are many forms to download we should need another menu structure. Another SMM could be useful here.
A survey for the students.	STF

Suppose now that we keep on with our meetings, where I keep on telling you what I want.

"I'd like to have a survey for the students, about their opinions about the subject, their suggestions etc. I don't want just a text file for them to print. I want them to fill it on-line. The results must be stored somewhere for me to retrieve them at my convenience"

This is just a very specific demand. We will need to have a database to work with this point…

"I'd also would like to have a set of on-line forms that they could use to enter all the personal data that the course and the school could ask them. I don't want to have hundreds of pieces of paper in my desk. I want a computer file with all the data I need about the students…"—I keep on saying.

Well, these demands require some kind of database work, so here is when we notice that we need to program some parts of the site in ASP.

So, here we've got another axiom valid for the professional programmers:

Programming in ASP is a task that emerges from the requests of the customer. As it takes time and effort to do it:

NEVER start an ASP page if it is not strictly necessary.

ASP is not a "toy". It is common that the inexpert programmer uses it to practice and to demonstrate his skills.

Terrible mistake: ASP will require much of his time, and will dramatically increase the budget of the project, so it will become more expensive and the development time will seem to be endless.

Remember that the professional programmer must **finish his work in time**. This is the golden rule of the programmer. The customer doesn't care about if the site has ASP pages or not. He just wants his site working on schedule.

So, the golden rules for the ASP programmers are:

Program in ASP as less as possible.

Make your ASP programs as simple as possible.

If you follow these simple rules, my friend, it doesn't matter if you are not an erudite that knows by hart all the ASP syntax: You will be a better professional programmer.

As I told the readers some chapters ago, I've been programming computers from more that fifteen years now, and I've seen the work of a lot of people: I just can't remember how many delayed projects I've seen just because some programmers thought it could be "cool" to do this, or to do that, to add this routine, to modify that one etc, etc.

Remember that the customer (and also your manager) generally don't understand what you did, so they are not able to value your work. They just look at the fact that you are delayed, so, the basic strategy is this one:

FIRST: Finish your work in the simplest and easiest possible way.

SECOND: Deliver it, or send it (to your boss, to the customer, to the one you have to report at office)

THIRD: Be sure you have been paid for it. Never make a work if you don't know if the customer is going to pay you to have done it.

FOURTH: Once and only once you have made steps 1 to 3 you can suggest your coolest ideas, and show your innovative personality. If the customer likes it, you'll have more work to do. If he doesn't, there is nothing to loose. Many inexpert programmers just put in practice their coolest ideas in the beginning, and without the authorization of the customer. Sometimes it works, but it is very common that this fact could be just perceived by him as a waste of time.

The ASP itself

Let's go back to our example. The customer has some demands that can only be satisfied with the use of a database. For us, database means ASP.

Every time we need to work with stored data we will need the services of an Active Server Page.

What is an ASP file?

Every text file that has an extension of .asp, will be considered as an ASP file. So, you can write ASP files using your favorite text editor, the same way as you program a standard HTML file.

In the next chapter, we will discuss the syntax of the language.

The first thing you have to know about ASP is that it exists in coordination with HTML, so you can place in the same file ASP instructions and HTML tags.

Example:

Create a file with your text editor and name it "first. asp"

Just write:

<HTML>Hello</HTML>

Save the file.

This is a valid ASP file. Any pure HTML file can be renamed from its original .htm extension to a .asp extension, and it will work.

The first problem is that it will only work in a ASP server!. This means that you have to publish it in the net to make them work. You have been told (some chapters ago), that before writing any single line of code, you have to subscribe to a hosting service, in order to place there your site.

You have to be sure that this service allows the publication of ASP pages in their servers. If you don't know how to do it, just use your Internet Browser and search for "Internet Hosting Service", or "Free Internet Hosting Services", as you prefer.

Any serious work for a customer must be placed in a paid Hosting Company. The free services place ads in your page every time you use them. However, they are useful to make personal pages or test sites of your works.

If you have a PC computer, there is a way that lets you simulate an ASP server in your local machine to make a proof of the ASP files before publishing them, using the Internet Information Server (IIS) package. [8]

This is worth if you have a dial-up connection with the net and you want to save money. (A dial-up connection uses telephone pulses to receive and send data to the net). However, the professional programmer has usually got a wide-range 24x365 connection (24 hours, 365 days) that lets them be connected to the net permanently, so the proofs are made in the net itself. The best proof is the proof made in real conditions.

The second thing you need is a FTP (File Transfer Protocol) program, that is used to send and receive data from the hosting server. It is easier than sending an e-mail. You just send the files, and they are automatically published in the other side. If you don't have a FTP program yet, you can buy one on the net, or download a free one. There are several sites where you can download free software, and in general you can find FTP programs there. In addition, many serious hosting services have a file or a page where they tell you how you have to setup the FTP program to access to their site and publish your files automatically.

---

[8] IIS comes with Windows, but must be installed separately. See your Windows Installation Guide to learn how to do it. As I don't like this method, I won't speak too much about it.

Summary:

In order to work with ASP you need:

1) A text editor

2) An Internet Browser.

3) A connection to Internet. It is better if you have a wide-range 24x365 line.

4) One FTP program

5) An agreement with a hosting service that allows you to place your page in their servers

6) The FTP program setup to send the files directly to the server. (That means configured to publish the files as soon as they are sent)

Dialects

ASP is a language that allows two dialects in it:

VBScript: Visual Basic script for ASP

Jscript: Java script for ASP

What does it mean?:

There are two groups of programmers: The ones that love Visual Basic and the ones that are used to program in C. (Java is similar to C). In order to catch both markets, there are two different ways you can place the commands: in a way that is similar to Visual Basic, that we will call VBScript, or in a way that is similar to Java, that we will call JScript.

My first idea was to teach both ways in this book, but I thought about it, and I changed my mind. My experience with my students showed me that it is extremely confusing for them to be learning both dialects at the same time, and the idea of this work is to make a book that could be as readable as possible, even if some commands have to be sacrificed. That's why I decided to focus the ASP part of the book in the VBScript dialect that is the easiest one. Once you know VBScript ASP and you have practiced with it, you will be able to learn Jscript easily. However, you will find it is worthless: Everything you need can be made with VBScript, so you don't need to know something else just to do the same things you already know.

Chapter 14

ASP Syntax

First steps in ASP:

The first thing you have to know about ASP is the sentence:

```
<Script Language=VBScript>
```

This command must be placed at the top of your page because it tells the server that you are using the Visual Basic Script dialect of ASP. If you don't place it, the server could start to think that you are using the Java Script dialect, so your commands won't be recognized as valid orders.

The second thing you have to know are the ASP tags "<%" and "%>".

When you want to place an ASP clause, you have to place them between the "<%" and "%>" tags.

Let's see the core commands of the language.

How to place text in a ASP page:

The command <% Response.Write("Text") %> lets you write any text in the page. In HTML you just have to write something, and it will be placed as it is. ASP, lets you also write normal text, but also lets you write the result of a mathematic or logic operation.

Example:

"2+2"

This is a literal text. It is just HTML. The page will show:

"2+2"

now look at this:

```
<%
x=2+2
response.write(x)
%>
```

This ASP commands will look in the page like this:

4

In other words, ASP calculated the sum of the numbers and placed the answer. As you see, it is a powerful tool to work with. Notice that we placed the sum in a variable. We do not just place 2+2, but x=2+2, that means that the variable X must have the value of 2 plus 2.

Let's see how it works with a text:

If we just write: "John" & "_" & "Doe" , the page will look like:

"John" & "_" & "Doe"

This is just HTML text and the page writes it as it is. However, if we convert it to ASP, we will have:

```
<%
x="John" & "_" & "Doe"
response.write(x)
%>
```

In ASP the "&" character works as a "+" character for texts, so it adds a text to the other. What we will see in the page is:

John _ Doe

ASP lets us manipulate strings of text as easy as numbers!

As **Response. Write** is a long command, we can just use a synonym that is **<%= %>**.

In other words: Having

<% X="John" & "_" & "Doe" %>

These sentences are equal:

<% response.write(X) %> is equal to **<%= X %>**

Publishing an ASP file in the Web

Let's now write our first combined HTML and ASP page.

It is easier to do it if you open the programs you'll need at the same time and you keep them opened in different windows. All you have to do is to navigate from window to window to do things faster.

So… Open your text editor, the internet browser, and the FTP program. Make it be ready to transmit.

1) Use your text editor, and create a file called "first.asp". FTP programs generally look for the files to send in a specific folder of your hard disk. Be

sure that the text editor will save your file directly in that folder. The process will be easier and faster if you just save your files in the same place where it will be searched to be sent.

2) Write:

```
<Script Language=VBScript>

<HTML>

<BODY>

<% X="John" & "_" & "Doe" %>

<%= X %>

</BODY>

</HTML>
```

3) Save the file.

4) Switch to your FTP program to send the file to the Hosting Server. (I suppose that you are always on-line so I don't have to tell you to connect your machine to the net each time you have to do something)

5) Switch to your Internet Explorer.

6) Type this address:

http://www.yourhosting.com/you/first.asp

where yourhosting.com means the address of the company where your page is located, and YOU is your personal folder. If your customer has a personal domain name (let's suppose it is TEACHER.COM), so you just have to type:

http://www.teacher.com/first.asp

You should see something like this:

John Doe

If you were able to do it: CONGRATULATIONS! You have made your first HTML/ASP file.

If you find difficult to follow these steps, don't worry. They are not so easy as it may seem. I had to spend some time and make several proofs until I could do it. It is normal. Be patient, try several times, and try to solve the problems that are presented the best you can.

It is impossible to describe here all the problems that may happen, but I will comment some of the most frequent ones:

Steps 1,2,3—Creating the file:

Some text editors create automatically .txt files. If you are using Microsoft Word[9] as a text editor, it will create a .doc file. This is not correct. Remember you have to create a .asp file. Check with your Windows Explorer [10] to see if you have created a .asp file. Be sure you know which is the folder that contains the file.

Print the .asp file in a sheet of paper and read it. Be sure the code is correctly written. Any error will make the file be unable to run.

Step 4 FTP program: The use of the FTP program must be learnt reading its user's manual. Each of them work in a similar way, but the specific commands are different, so get one of them and try. In general, you have to setup these items:

---

[9] Microsoft Word is a trade mark of Microsoft Corp.

[10] Windows Explorer is a trade mark of Microsoft Corp.

a) What is the folder of your hard disk that contains the files to be sent. This is usually called "Local Directory". For example: If you have a folder called "page" at "C:", you will have to place "C:\page"

b) Where must the files be sent to. The ftp address must be sent to you by the company that gives you a hosting service. In general they will give you an address that is something like: "ftp.yourhostingservice.com"

c) Your user name and password. The company will also give you a user name and a password.

Once you have done these steps correctly, all you have to do is to run the ftp program, log in placing your username and password, select the file(s) you want to publish and then click in the appropriate button. Your file(s) will be sent and published in your Internet Site immediately. If you still have problems, mail their support department (if you have bought the software), or try to get another program (if you downloaded a free copy of a program)

Steps 5,6: Viewing the published ASP page in your explorer: Be sure that you are typing the correct address of your page. Perhaps it is something like:

http://yourdomainname.com/first.asp

However, some hosting companies place your work in an inner folder, so perhaps you have to write something like this:

http://yourdomainname.com/userfolder/first.asp

Warning: Some internet addresses need the "www" after the http://, and some others don't.

Perhaps you need to write:

http://www.yourdomainname.com/first.asp

As I told you before, perhaps you will have to make some failed attempts to publish your page before you succeed.

ASP usual structures:

Date commands

You can create a variable that contains the actual Date, month, day , year etc. Let's see how we do it

---

X=#01/01/1980# ' The variable X has a date value. Notice that we have place the value between numerals (#)

X=Date() ' The variable X has the actual date as value

X=Now() ' The variable X has the actual date and hour as value

X=WeekDay(Now()) ' The variable X has the actual day of the week as value

X=Day(Date()) ' The variable X has the actual day as value

X=month(Date()) ' The variable X has the actual month as value

X=year(Date()) ' The variable X has the actual year as value

For/Next structure

The first structure we are going to see is the loop structure:

Every Basic and Visual Basic programmer knows the For/Next structures of the language. Well, you've also got then here.

You can repeat whatever it is between FOR and NEXT the number of times you want.

Example:

```
<%
<Script Language=VBScript>
X=0 'variable x has an initial value of zero
For I=1 to 100 'Everything that is placed from here up to the "next" sentence must be done 100 times
X=x+1 'The value of X must be replaced by X+1. It is accumulative.
Next ' Up to here
Response.Write(X)
%>
```

When you execute this program, the page will show the value of "100", because we told the computer to add one to a variable with value=0 one hundred times.

If/Then Structure:

The next structure we are going to see is the conditional structure or If/then structure. (also called if/then/else)

The If/then structure is used to make bifurcations in the program. Suppose you want a program that could be able to show a different message depending of the day of the week. You should tell the machine something like this:

My birthday is in January, so if we are in December , I'd like that the following message could be seen in the page:

"My Birthday is next month"

As we already know, Date() will give us the current date.

```
<%

<Script Language=VBScript>

X=date() 'variable x has an initial value of the current date

If month(X)=12 then 'If the month is 12, we are in December

Response.Write("My birthday is next month")

End if

%>
```

Do while structure

It is similar to the For/next structure. However you cannot place here a number of iterations, but a logical condition. If you place a logical clause that is logically TRUE, you can ask ASP to do the loop until the condition is FALSE.

This clause is very useful when you search into databases, because you can ask it to do it until it comes to the end of it.

First of all, there are two very useful clauses:

.EOF ' indicates the END OF FILE of a table or recordset

.BOF ' indicates the BEGINNING OF FILE of a table or recordset. A recordset is a logical view of the physical table. We will see in detail the differences between tables and recordsets later.

Example: suppose you want to count the records of the "RS" Recordset. You can do it this way:

```
<%

<Script Language=VBScript>

counter=0 ' variable counter is set to zero

Do while NOT RS.EOF 'you always start on top of the recordset. This loop
continues until the End of File of it is found.

RS.MoveNext 'jumps one record below

Counter=counter+1 ' Adds one to the variable counter each time the loop
comes to this place

Loop ' Final part of the Do while clause

Response.Write(Counter) ' Prints the final value of the variable, that is
the number of records of the recordset


%>
```

Select Case Structure

It works as a kind of concatenation of if/then commands.

Example:

```
<%
<Script Language=VBScript>
X=WeekDay(Now()) 'variable x has an initial value of the day of the week
Select Case(X)
Case 1 : Response.write("Today is Sunday")
Case 2 : Response.write("Today is Monday")
...
Case 7 : Response.write("Today is Saturday")
End Select
%>
```

ASP Environment Variables

The environment variables can be used to control and inform of the status of the session, and to open databases and tables.

Example:

If you want to track the number of visitors on-line that are visiting the page, just add this line in your main page (if it is a standard HTML file, you should rename it as .asp)

```
<% Application("Users") =Application("Users")+1 %>
```

When you want to know how many people are there connected, you just write:

```
<HTML><BODY>
Now there are <%=Application("Users")%> users connected !
</BODY></HTML>
```

Notice that we are mixing the HTML code and the ASP commands. Remember that all the file must be an ASP file .asp (All ASP files allows the use of HTML clauses in them).

The page will look like:

```
Now there are 25 users connected !
```

Opening Databases

We have been talking about databases in the past chapters. We said that a database is the way you've got to store data in the hard disk of the server. A database can be seen as a group of tables. For example, a typical commercial enterprise can have its corporate database, that consists in the tables "Payroll", "Customers", "Accountancy", "Personal", "Projects" etc.

Each table can be seen as a group of files (or columns) of a related nature. For example, the table "Payroll" may have the columns "ID", "First name", "Last Name", "Address", "e-mail" , etc.

We call "fields" to the columns of a table and "records" to the rows.

However, we do not work directly with the tables, but with the "**Recordsets**". A recordset is a logic structure, a copy, a "mirror" of the table that we use as a working platform. A recordset can be a literal copy of the table, with all the fields and rows, or a reduced version of it. If we know that we are not going to work with the entire table, but with one or two fields, it is easier and faster to create a recordset that contains just the fields we are going to use. A recordset can be a query of the original table.

For example, we can create a Recordset from the table "Payroll" with all the employees that have a salary that is less than $12000 per year.

Going back to ASP, if you want to open a database, or a recordset, you have to use the "Server" environment variable with the properties "CreateObject", and "MapPath"

Example:

The following lines open the dbempremovil.mdb Access Database. You have to assign the result to a variable. (in this case DB1). DRI is a temporary variable that we create to store the information about the driver that ASP must use to open it. If you want to use other kind of databases, as SQL or DBF files you have to look at the ADODB drivers that you have installed in your machine. In this book I will use Access databases, but you have to have in mind that if you want to use another one, you only have to change the following command, and VOILA! , it is ready. ASP is a very powerful language that lets you change the environment of your database modifying just a few lines of code.

```
Set DB1 = Server.CreateObject("ADODB.Connection")

Dri="DRIVER=Microsoft Access Driver (*.mdb);DBQ="
Dri= Dri & Server.MapPath("dbempremovil.mdb")
DB1.Open Dri
```

To open a recordset, we also have to use the "Server" environment variable. The following example opens it and assigns the result to a variable called RS1 (Recordset one). You have to create them AFTER you have opened the database.

```
Set RS1 = Server.CreateObject("ADODB.Recordset")
```

We will call this structure as a Standard Query Module (SQM).

The only thing you have to change when you want to open another database is the name of the .mdb file and the name of the variables (DB1 and RS1 in this case). If you use the same names for more than a recordset, perhaps the ASP will be confused, so a wide range of errors could happen. It is safer if you just use a different variable for each recordset you are using. In the appendix section we've got a SQM source code.

In the next chapter we will see how to work with databases using ASP.

CHAPTER 15

USING DATABASES

Once we have learnt how to open databases, we must see how to store and retrieve data from them.

We have seen that a file must start with a SQM module, that opens the database and the recordset.

After it, we must "fill" the recordset with the data we need.

We must use a SQL statement to do this: (SQL is the most popular language for database queries in the world. ASP just uses this syntax)

Example:

Suppose we have opened the database and a recordset called RS1. We've got a table called "Students" with the fields [ID], [name], [address], [age], [e-mail], etc . If we want to work with the data of some particular students, we can make a filter using the names. If we want to have the records of the students with name="smith", we should write:

> "SELECT * FROM Students WHERE [name]='smith' ORDER BY [name]"

A typical SQL instruction is written as:

> SELECT * FROM **table name** WHERE [**field**]='**a value**' ORDER BY [**field**]

However, this sentence must be assigned to a variable. Look at this:

```
Tquery="SELECT * FROM Students WHERE [name]='smith' ORDER
BY [name]"
```

Here we have assigned to the variable Tquery the SQL statement.

To activate the recordset, we call it this way:

```
RS1.Open TQuery, DB1
```

Where DB1 is variable we used when we opened the database.

So, the complete SQL module (including the instructions to open a recordset) is:

```
Set DB1 = Server.CreateObject("ADODB.Connection")
Dri="DRIVER=Microsoft Access Driver (*.mdb);DBQ="
Dri= Dri & Server.MapPath("dbempremovil.mdb")
DB1.Open Dri

Set RS1 = Server.CreateObject("ADODB.Recordset")
TQuery="SELECT * FROM Students  WHERE [name]='smith' ORDER
BY [name]"
RS1.Open TQuery, DB1
```

If you have many smiths in your classroom, you won't be able to identify a single student. That's why it is preferred to work with the Ids rather than using the names of the students.

We could use the SQL sentence:

```
TQuery="SELECT * FROM Students  WHERE [ID]='25' "
```

If we know that the ID of Mr. Smith is '25', and we ask for the student whose ID is '25', we will just get the record of Mr. Smith ("our" Smith, the one we want)

Well, once we have located a record in a database, we might want to show it. To print the contents of a field in the page we use a command we already now: Response.Write (or <%=).

A sentence could be:

<HTML><BODY> Student ID: <%=RS1("ID")%> </BODY> </HTML>

This command, tells ASP to print the contents of the field "ID" of the current record. As the SQL sentence says it is just the record of Mr. Smith, the page will look like:

Student ID: 25

, where '25' is the data stored in the database.

By the way: Look the way we are mixing HTML and ASP!

Remember that they both work together, we write the text in HTML, and we retrieve the data using ASP.

Sending data to an ASP file

We have to learn now how to tell ASP which is the data we want to search. In the previous paragraphs, we've seen how to make the SQL sentence look for the record of Mr. Smith. However, the user can't write the ASP code; he just types the value in the page, and ASP takes it.

In order to do this, we have to use a combination of HTML and ASP commands. This structure is called a "FORM". An ASP/HTML form is the proper way to let the user type what he wants to search, open the database, make the right SQL statement, find the data and expose it in the page.

In order to do that, we have to define the concept of a parameter. The values that the user types in the pages must be introduced in the system to let SQL make the statement. We will call these vales a "parameter". When you call an ASP page, you can attach to the call one or more parameters, that are introduced in the code of the page.

The ASP clause **Request.Form("data")** is used to store any value sent to it as a parameter.

Example:

```
X=request.form("name")
```

This instruction stores the value of the parameter "name" in a variable called "X".

In other words, the sequence of an ASP/HTML form is this:

- The HTML section of the page asks the user to type a value.

- The user types something and presses ENTER.

- When he does it, an ASP page is called with that data converted in parameters.

- This ASP page uses this parameters as part of their code, and does the database search and print.

As a matter of fact, you can use two files (one HTML file, and one ASP file), or just one ASP file that calls itself, so it is reloaded with the parameters.

Let's see how we do that:

Creating an ASP/HTML Form:

This is the part that can be located in a HTML file.

File form.html that loads students.asp

```
<FORM ACTION="students.asp" NAME="formpmc"
METHOD="POST" target=mainframe>
<p><font size="1">Introduce Student ID:</font></p>
<INPUT TYPE="TEXT" NAME="ID" VALUE="" >
<INPUT TYPE="SUBMIT" NAME="submit1" VALUE="Press Here to
Submit" >
<INPUT TYPE="RESET" NAME="Reset1" VALUE="Reset" >
```

This file calls the "students.asp" file, that is our ASP file.

Let's look at the form structure:

The sentence FORM ACTION="file" opens the form and sends what the users type to "file". In this case everything that is typed by the user will be sent to "students.asp".

Remember that we were using a three framed structure? The command TARGET=mainframe also orders the file to load in the third frame, that was called "mainframe".

The INPUT TYPE="TEXT" command creates a dialog box, where the user is allowed to write data.

The INPUT TYPE="SUBMIT" command creates a button that must be pressed to enter the data.

The INPUT TYPE="RESET" command creates a button that clears the data placed in the dialog box before it was sent. It is useful if you made a typing mistake and you want to start again.

The page will look like this:

Introduce Student ID: [   ]

Press Here to Submit RESET

As you can see, the result is alright, but the form needs alignment.

We can work with a table, just to place the text wherever we want. The structure would be:

```
<FORM ACTION="students.asp" NAME="formpmc" METHOD="POST"
target=mainframe>
<TABLE><TR>
<TD><p><font size="1">Introduce Student ID:</font></p></TD>
<TD><INPUT TYPE="TEXT" NAME="ID" VALUE="" ></TD>
</TR><TR>
<TD><INPUT TYPE="SUBMIT" NAME="submit1" VALUE="Press Here to
Submit" ></TD>
<TD><INPUT TYPE="RESET"  NAME="Reset1" VALUE="Reset" ></TD>
</TR></TABLE>
```

The page now will look like this:

Introduce Student ID: [   ]

    Press Here to Submit   **RESET**

This is the HTML part of the Form Structure.

If we want to work with only one file that reloads itself with the value of the parameter, we can work directly with the "students.asp". Here the code changes a bit. Look at this:

File students.asp that reloads itself

```
<% studentID=Request.Form("ID") %>

<% if studentID=null then %>
<FORM ACTION="students.asp" NAME="formpmc"
METHOD="POST" target=mainframe>
<p><font size="1">Introduce Student ID:</font></p>
<INPUT TYPE="TEXT" NAME="ID" VALUE="" >
<INPUT TYPE="SUBMIT" NAME="submit1" VALUE="Press Here to
Submit" >
<INPUT TYPE="RESET" NAME="Reset1" VALUE="Reset" >

<% else %>

'Here it goes the search part.

<% end if %>
```

The clause NULL means that a variable is empty.

The ASP file starts requesting for a variable "ID". The first time we call it no value was sent, so the variable "studentID" has a value=null.

The IF/THEN clause checks this and writes the form. When the user types and sends the data, the file calls itself (it calls students.asp, that is itself), but this time it will have attached a value for the variable "ID". This second time, the value that the user typed is stored in the variable "studentID", so the IF/THEN clause is false. The instructions that are placed between the IF and the ELSE are ignored, so the FORM structure is not shown to the user, and the program just executes the part of the program that is placed between the ELSE and the END IF sections.

If we place the SQM module between the ELSE and the END IF sections, we'll have:

```
<% studentID=Request.Form("ID") %>

<% if studentID=null then %>
<FORM ACTION="students.asp" NAME="formpmc"
METHOD="POST" target=mainframe>
<p><font size="1">Introduce Student ID:</font></p>
<INPUT TYPE="TEXT" NAME="ID" VALUE="" >
<INPUT TYPE="SUBMIT" NAME="submit1" VALUE="Press Here
to Submit" >
<INPUT TYPE="RESET"  NAME="Reset1" VALUE="Reset" >

<% else %>
<%
Set DB1 = Server.CreateObject("ADODB.Connection")
Dri="DRIVER=Microsoft Access Driver (*.mdb);DBQ="
Dri= Dri & Server.MapPath("dbempremovil.mdb")
DB1.Open Dri

Set RS1 = Server.CreateObject("ADODB.Recordset")
TQuery="SELECT * FROM Students  WHERE [ID]=studentID
ORDER BY [name]"
RS1.Open TQuery, DB1
%>
Student ID:  <%=RS1("ID")%>
<% end if %>
```

This is the standard structure we will use to search and display data stored in a database.

As a matter of fact, we could insert a <table> structure in it just to view the fields in a proper order.

The code would be something like this:

```asp
<% studentID=Request.Form("ID") %>

<% if studentID=null then %>
<FORM ACTION="students.asp" NAME="formpmc"
METHOD="POST" target=mainframe>
<p><font size="1">Introduce Student ID:</font></p>
<INPUT TYPE="TEXT" NAME="ID" VALUE="" >
<INPUT TYPE="SUBMIT" NAME="submit1" VALUE="Press Here
to Submit" >
<INPUT TYPE="RESET" NAME="Reset1" VALUE="Reset" >

<% else %>
<%
Set DB1 = Server.CreateObject("ADODB.Connection")
Dri="DRIVER=Microsoft Access Driver (*.mdb);DBQ="
Dri= Dri & Server.MapPath("dbempremovil.mdb")
DB1.Open Dri

Set RS1 = Server.CreateObject("ADODB.Recordset")
TQuery="SELECT * FROM Students WHERE [ID]=studentID ORDER
BY [name]"
RS1.Open TQuery, DB1
%>
<table>
<tr>
<td>Student ID: <%=RS1("ID")%> </td>
<td> Name: <%=RS1("name")%> </td>
<td> Age: <%=RS1("age")%> </td>
</tr><tr>
<td>Address: <%=RS1("address")%> </td>
<td>E-mail: <%=RS1("e-mail")%> </td>
</tr><table>

<% end if %>
```

The first time, the page will look like this:

```
┌─────────────────────────────────────────────────────────┐
│                                                           │
│  Student ID:    [          ]                              │
│                                                           │
│  ┌──────────────┐      ┌──────────┐                       │
│  │ Press here to│      │ Reset    │                       │
│  │ submit       │      │          │                       │
│  └──────────────┘      └──────────┘                       │
└─────────────────────────────────────────────────────────┘
```

When the page reloads itself, it will look like this:

```
┌─────────────────────────────────────────────────────────┐
│                                                           │
│  Student ID: [ 25   ]  Name: [ John   ]   Age: [ 18    ]  │
│                                                           │
│  Address:    [ xxxxxx ] e-mail [ js@xx ]                  │
└─────────────────────────────────────────────────────────┘
```

So, we will call this structure as a standard search and display module (SSDM).

Each time we have to search data in a database and then show the results in the page we will use a SSDM.

Storing data on-line

The previous module lets us watch what the database contains. However, someone has to fill it. In our example, the students are supposed to enter their data on-line, so we must see the way we use to store data in the database, from the forms that the user fills. We will adapt SSDM to store data instead of showing it. The sequence is this:

The first time we load the ASP file, no parameters are passed to it, so the FORM appears and the student has to fill the dialog boxes with his data. When he submits the form, the file reloads itself, but this time there are parameters passed, so the FORM is not shown, and the ASP file just adds them into the database.

In order to do that, we have to replace the "SELECT… " SQL sentence for something like this one:

INSERT INTO students (ID,name,address,age,e-mail) VALUES

('5',"John Smith",'5 peanut road', '18', 'js@uba.com')

Where:

- "INSERT INTO" and "VALUES" are the specific SQL commands.

- "Students" is the name of the table

- (ID,name,address,age,e-mail) are the fields of the table.

- ('5',"John Smith", … are the values that we want to insert in the table.

However, remember that the first time we execute the page a form appears and the student fills it and submits it, so they are converted in parameters that the page loads when it self-reloads.

So, we've got parameters that have to be converted in a string of characters of the type:

("value"; "value"; "value"; "value").

Remember we use the following ASP clause to retrieve a parameter:

"Request.Form("parameter")"

The first part of the ASP file is similar to the previous example:

Create a ASP file called "loadstudent.asp", and write:

Loadstudent.asp (first part)

```
<% studentID      =Request.Form("ID") %>
<% studentname    =Request.Form("name") %>
<% studentad=Request.Form("address") %>
<% studentage     =Request.Form("age") %>
<% studentemail   =Request.Form("email") %>


<% if studentID=null then %>
<FORM ACTION="loadstudent.asp" NAME="formpmc"
METHOD="POST" target=mainframe>
<p><font size="1">Introduce Student ID:</font></p>

<INPUT TYPE="TEXT" NAME="ID"       VALUE="" >
<INPUT TYPE="TEXT" NAME="name"     VALUE="" >
<INPUT TYPE="TEXT" NAME="address"  VALUE="" >
<INPUT TYPE="TEXT" NAME="age"      VALUE="" >
<INPUT TYPE="TEXT" NAME="email"    VALUE="" >

<INPUT TYPE="SUBMIT" NAME="submit1" VALUE="Press Here
to Submit" >
<INPUT TYPE="RESET"  NAME="Reset1" VALUE="Reset" >

<% else %>

'Here goes the INSERT INTO… statement

<% end if %>
```

So, the first time the parameter studentID is null, so the FORM will be displayed. The student will fill it in, and will submit it. The page reloads itself, but this time studentID is not null, so the form is not shown and the INSERT INTO section is executed.

Creating the INSERT INTO String:

As any other SQL statement, the INSERT INTO clause must be assigned to a variable, so first of all we have to create a variable that contains these values:

> INSERT INTO students (ID,name,address,age,e-mail) VALUES
>
> ('5',"John Smith",'5 peanut road', '18', 'js@uba.com')

It could be something like:

> X= " INSERT INTO students (ID,name,address,age,e-mail) VALUES
>
> ('5',"John Smith",'5 peanut road', '18', 'js@uba.com') "

However, it is not so easy to do it. We have no problem with the first part (up to the first parenthesis after the VALUE command):

> X= " INSERT INTO students (ID,name,address,age,e-mail) VALUES "

Now: '5',"John Smith",'5 peanut road', '18', 'js@uba.com' are stored in the initial parameters ID,name,address,age,e-mail.

We have to place them between brackets and separated by a comma. Let's use the "XX" temporary variable to do this. To create a string of the type 'xx','xx','xx' we must use the "&" operator , that is the equivalent of the "+" operator for strings. The brackets and commas must be placed as an initial string " ,' " and a final string " ', " .

So:

Initial= " , "

Final= " ' , "

StudentID   = "(' " & studentID & final

Studentname   =initial & studentID & final

Studentad   =initial & studentad & final

Studentage   =initial & studentage & final

Studentemail   =initial & studentemail & " ')"

If we make just one string called "allstudents"

allstudents= studentID & studentname & studentad & studentage & studentmail

The variable allstudents has now the form:

('5',"John Smith",'5 peanut road', '18', 'js@uba.com')

If we already had a variable X with the value:

X= " INSERT INTO students (ID,name,address,age,e-mail) VALUES "

And now we do:

SQL=X & allstudents

We finish with a variable SQL that has the SQL statement as a result.

We just have to execute it with the clause:

xct=BD1.Execute SQL

As a last step, we can add a Link that says "Insertion Done. Press here to continue"

Loadstudent.asp (complete)

```asp
<% studentID      =Request.Form("ID") %>
<% studentname    =Request.Form("name") %>
<% studentad=Request.Form("address") %>
<% studentage     =Request.Form("age") %>
<% studentemail   =Request.Form("email") %>


<% if studentID=null then %>
<FORM ACTION="loadstudent.asp" NAME="formpmc"
METHOD="POST" target=mainframe>
<p><font size="1">Introduce Student ID:</font></p>

<INPUT TYPE="TEXT" NAME="ID"        VALUE="" >
<INPUT TYPE="TEXT" NAME="name"      VALUE="" >
<INPUT TYPE="TEXT" NAME="address"   VALUE="" >
<INPUT TYPE="TEXT" NAME="age"       VALUE="" >
<INPUT TYPE="TEXT" NAME="email"     VALUE="" >

<INPUT TYPE="SUBMIT" NAME="submit1" VALUE="Press Here to
Submit" >
<INPUT TYPE="RESET"  NAME="Reset1" VALUE="Reset" >

<% else %>

<%
Set DB1 = Server.CreateObject("ADODB.Connection")
Dri="DRIVER=Microsoft Access Driver (*.mdb);DBQ="
Dri= Dri & Server.MapPath("dbempremovil.mdb")
DB1.Open Dri
```

```
Set RS1 = Server.CreateObject("ADODB.Recordset")
TQuery="SELECT * FROM Students  ORDER BY [name]"
RS1.Open TQuery, DB1
%>



Initial= " ,' "

Final= " ', "

StudentID          = "( ' "   & studentID & final

Studentname      =initial & studentID & final

Studentad                       =initial & studentad & final

Studentage          =initial & studentage & final

Studentemail      =initial & studentemail & " ' )"

Allstudents= studentID & studentname & studentad & studentage &
studentmail

SQL= " INSERT INTO students  (ID,name,address,age,e-mail)  VALUES

" & Allstudents

xct=BD1.Execute SQL

%><a href="index.html>Insertion Done. Press here to continue</a><%
<% end if %>
```

This is the standard structure we are going to use for Storing data in the databases taken from on-line forms. We will call it Standard Input Module (SIM)

Modifying Stored data:

If you want to edit or modify the data stored in the table "students" , all you have to do is to replace the "INSERT INTO" clause by the SQL "UPDATE / SET" instruction.

You can use a SIM module and just replace the SQL variable by an order that says:

> **UPDATE** (TABLE) **SET** (FIELD)="VALUE" **WHERE**
> (FIELD)="VALUE"

What does it mean? (TABLE) is the name of the table you want to modify.

SET (FIELD) is the name of the field of that table that will be replaced.

(FIELD)="VALUE" is value that will be stored in the field.

WHERE (FIELD): You have to set a criteria to make a valid modification. The machine has to understand which is the record that has to be change. If we use the "ID" field to place the criteria, the machine will understand that you want to change the name of the person whose ID=25, for example.

(FIELD)="VALUE" The final sentence is the value that the criteria field must have (In this case is 25)

In the SIM modules, the "VALUES" are stored in parameters that can be read with the clause "Request.Form", so the complete order looks like this:

```
SQL="UPDATE students SET name='" &
Request.Form("Studentname") & "' WHERE ID=" &
Request.form("StudentID")

IRS=TConnect.Execute(SQL)
```

Here is the complete module:

Modifystudent.asp (complete)

```
<% studentID      =Request.Form("ID") %>
<% studentname    =Request.Form("name") %>
<% studentad=Request.Form("address") %>
<% studentage     =Request.Form("age") %>
<% studentemail   =Request.Form("email") %>


<% if studentID=null then %>
<FORM ACTION="modifystudent.asp" NAME="formpmc"
METHOD="POST" target=mainframe>
<p><font size="1">Introduce Student ID:</font></p>

<INPUT TYPE="TEXT" NAME="ID"        VALUE="" >
<INPUT TYPE="TEXT" NAME="name"      VALUE="" >
<INPUT TYPE="TEXT" NAME="address"   VALUE="" >
<INPUT TYPE="TEXT" NAME="age"       VALUE="" >
<INPUT TYPE="TEXT" NAME="email"     VALUE="" >

<INPUT TYPE="SUBMIT" NAME="submit1" VALUE="Press Here
to Submit" >
<INPUT TYPE="RESET"  NAME="Reset1" VALUE="Reset" >

<% else %>

<%
Set DB1 = Server.CreateObject("ADODB.Connection")
Dri="DRIVER=Microsoft Access Driver (*.mdb);DBQ="
Dri= Dri & Server.MapPath("dbempremovil.mdb")
DB1.Open Dri
```

```
Set RS1 = Server.CreateObject("ADODB.Recordset")
TQuery="SELECT * FROM Students  WHERE [ID]=" &
Request.Form("ID") & "ORDER BY [name]"
RS1.Open TQuery, DB1
%>

SQL="UPDATE students SET name='" &
Request.Form("Studentname")  &  "' WHERE ID=" &
Request.form("StudentID")


xct=BD1.Execute SQL

%><a href="index.html>Modification Done. Press here to
continue</a><%
<% end if %>

<% end if %>
```

We will call this structure a SEM Standard Edition Module

Deleting Records from the database:

The last thing we have to see is how to delete records. At this point of the book, it will be seen as something very easy. We just have to substitute the "UPDATE" statement by a "DELETE" SQL instruction:

```
DELETE FROM Students WHERE [ID]='25'
```

As the ID value was submitted as a parameter, so the instruction becomes:

"DELETE FROM Students WHERE [ID]='" & Request.form("ID") & "'"

Here is the complete module:

Erasestudent.asp (complete)

```
<% studentID=Request.Form("ID") %>

<% if studentID=null then %>
<FORM ACTION="students.asp" NAME="formpmc"
METHOD="POST" target=mainframe>
<p><font size="1">Introduce Student ID:</font></p>
<INPUT TYPE="TEXT" NAME="ID" VALUE="" >
<INPUT TYPE="SUBMIT" NAME="submit1" VALUE="Press Here
to Submit" >
<INPUT TYPE="RESET"  NAME="Reset1" VALUE="Reset" >

<% else %>
<%
Set DB1 = Server.CreateObject("ADODB.Connection")
Dri="DRIVER=Microsoft Access Driver (*.mdb);DBQ="
Dri= Dri & Server.MapPath("dbempremovil.mdb")
DB1.Open Dri

Set RS1 = Server.CreateObject("ADODB.Recordset")
TQuery="SELECT * FROM Students  WHERE [ID]=" & studentID "
RS1.Open TQuery, DB1
%>
<% SQL="DELETE FROM Students WHERE [ID]='" & StudentID &
"'"

xct=BD1.Execute SQL

%><a href="index.html>The record has been erased. Press here to
continue</a><%

<% end if %>
```

We can call this module a SDM (standard Deletion Module)

Well, this ends the basic training about ASP. The idea of this first book is to show the aspects related to HTML and to introduce you to the world of ASP, and that objective has been made.

For the ones who are interested in a deeper approach to the programming techniques in ASP, I suggest the reading of the second part of this book, that focuses in the tricks and professional ASP programming of the site.

I hope the lecture of this book could have been useful to you.

EPILOGUE

What's next now?

In these two books of the serial I've tried to show you the basic steps to build a site. The idea of the work was to go straight to the point, to show you the specific knowledge you need to create an ASP/HTML page, and to make emphasis in the development of a real site.

As a matter of fact, the site is so real that I still use it to manage the relationships with my students. Most of this site has been shown you here. You've even got the source codes of the pages to download them if you want.

All the relevant parts of the HTML have been discussed here, and the basics of ASP have been shown too. I think that with the knowledge you've got now, we have come to a good point to stop this first book.

Some of the readers may feel they want to go deeper. For them, the second book of this serial was thought. I was really doubting about what could be better: To write just one big (and more expensive) book with all the contents in it or to make two smaller (and less expensive) books:

One for the readers that just want to have an idea of the theme, and a second one for the ones who want to know more.

I decided that the readers of the first group shouldn't have to pay more for something they didn't want, so I preferred the alternative of the two books. This is also the reason why this books will only appear in paperback. The editor is able to publish them in hardcover, but this fact increases the prize of the books, so I will tell them I just want it to appear in the accessible paperback format.

Appendix

Source codes of the pages and examples shown in this book

Appendix:

As the title of the book remarks, this book is based on a real Internet Site. The page of the course of professor Marcelo Bosque is published in the net at http://www5.domaindlx.com/mgbosq/

There you can find (and download) the examples shown in this work. As Prof. Bosque teaches at University of Buenos Aires, the page is prepared to be consulted by his students. It is not the UBA institutional page, but Prof. Bosque courses' page. The real page has the text translated to Spanish, for obvious reasons (I remark that is a real site in activity). However, the source code is the same, because HTML and ASP statements are written in English.

BONUS!: As the site is in activity, new options are included to the site constantly!. This means that you have periodically more material and more examples of source code to download. The Site contains all you've seen here plus more!

Note: Prof. Bosque uses domaindlx.com as a hosting service but he has no relationship with them.

SOURCE CODE OF THE EXAMPLES SEEN IN THE BOOK

styles.css.

(CSS setup file)

You can download the source code free from
http://www5.domaindlx.com/mgbosq/estilos.css

Select the option "view source code" in your explorer and then copy &
paste the code to your computer.

```
P                {font-family: Verdana, Arial, Helvetica}
A:hover          {COLOR:lightgreen }
A                {color:#D3D3D3}
FONT             {color:white ;Font-family: Verdana, Arial,
Helvetica, sans-serif ; font-size:8pt }
.Title2          {color:white ; font-family: Monotype Corsiva;
Arial, Helvetica;font-size: 14pt; line-height: 12pt; font-
weight:bold;text-align: left }
BODY             {color:white ; Background-color:
rgb(102,102,153) ; font-family: Verdana, Arial, Helvetica }
.boton           {border-color: black ; font-size: 14pt ; border-
style:ridge ; border-left: none ; border-top: none}
.innertable      {color:#0066cc ; Background-color:lightyellow;
Border-color:grey}
.Title           {color:steelblue ; font-family: Monotype
Corsiva; Arial, Helvetica ; font-size: 18pt; line-height: 12pt ; font-
weight:bold; text-align: center}
```

Main.prg.

(Part of the SMM module)

You can download the source code free from
http://www5.domaindlx.com/mgbosq/main.htm

Select the option "view source code" in your explorer and then copy & paste the code to your computer.

```html
<html>
<head>
<meta http-equiv="Content-Language" content="en">
<meta http-equiv="Content-Type" content="text/html; charset =windows-1252">
<meta name="GENERATOR" content="youreditor">
<meta name="ProgId" content="youreditor.Document">
<title>main. html</title>
<STYLE type=text/css>@import URL("styles.css");</STYLE>
</head>
<body bgcolor="#FFFFCC">
<table border="0" width="100%">
 <tr><td ><img border="0" src="logo.gif" width="100" height="105"></td>
<td > <p align="left"><b><font size="1" face="Arial">University
name</font></b></p>
<p align="left"><b><font size="1" face="Arial">School name</font></b></p>
```

```
<p align="left"><b><font size="1" face="Arial">Subject name</font></b></p>

</td>

<td >   <p align="left"><b><font size="1" face="Arial">Valid for the course
of:</font></b></p>

<p align="left"><b><font size="1" face="Arial">Marcelo
Bosque</font></b></p>

</td></tr></table>

<table border="0" width="75%" height="155" align=center>

  <tr> <td width="75%" background="fce.jpg" height="250">

<p align="center"><b><font color="#FFFFCC" size="6">Contents of the
course</font></b></p>

<p align="left"><b><font color="#FFFFCC" size="5">Schedule</font></b></p>

<p align="left"><b><font color="#FFFFCC" size="5">Students
Records</font></b></p>

</td></tr></table>

<p align="left"><font size="2">Webmaster: (You)</font></p>

</body></html>
```

index.html.

(Part of the SMM module)

You can download the source code from
http://www5.domaindlx.com/mgbosq/index.html

Select the option "view source code" in your explorer and then copy &
paste the code to your computer.

```
<HTML>

<HEAD>

<TITLE>index.html</TITLE>

<META http-equiv=Content-Type content="text/html; charset=windows-1252">

<META content="your editor" name= GENERATOR>

<STYLE type=text/css>@import URL("styles.css");</STYLE>

</HEAD>

<FRAMESET border=false frameSpacing=0 rows=100,* frameBorder=0>

<FRAME name=topr marginWidth=0 marginHeight=0
src="menuhori.htm"  scrolling=no >

<FRAMESET cols=173,*>

<FRAME name=menu marginWidth=0 marginHeight=0
src="menuvertical.htm" scrolling=yes >

<FRAME name=mainframe src="main.htm"> </FRAMESET>
```

```
<NOFRAMES>

<p>This page uses frames but your explorer does not allow them</p>

</NOFRAMES>

</FRAMESET>

</HTML>
```

menuvertical.htm.

(Part of the SMM module)

You can download the source code from
http://www5.domaindlx.com/mgbosq/menuvertical.htm

Select the option "view source code" in your explorer and then copy &
paste the code to your computer.

```
<HTML>

<HEAD>

<TITLE>menuvertical.htm</TITLE>

<META http-equiv=Content-Type content="text/html; charset=iso-8859-1">

<STYLE type=text/css>@import URL("estilos.css");</STYLE>

<META content="youreditor" name=GENERATOR>

<META content="Marcelo-2003" name=AUTHOR>

</HEAD>

<BODY >

<TABLE width="99%" align=center  border=1>

<tr><TD  height=14 align="center"><FONT><a target="_top"
ref="indexit.html">Home</a></FONT></TD></tr>

<tr><TD  height=14 align="center"><FONT><a target="mainframe"
href="crono2003.htm"> Schedule</a> </FONT></TD></tr>
```

```
<tr><TD  height=14 align="center"><FONT><A target=_top
href="indexpublish.html">Publications</A></FONT> </TD> </tr>

<tr><TD  height=14 align="center"><FONT><a target="menu"
href="menuvertalu.htm"> Students</a>  </FONT></TD></tr>

<tr> <TD  height=14 align="center"><FONT><A target=mainframe
href="trabajoinv.htm"> Student's Research Works</A></FONT></TD>
</tr>




</TABLE>

</BODY>

</HTML>
```

menuhori.htm.

(Part of the SMM module)

You can download the source code from
http://www5.domaindlx.com/mgbosq/menuhori.htm

Select the option "view source code" in your explorer and then copy &
paste the code to your computer.

```
<HTML><HEAD><TITLE>menuhori</TITLE>

<META http-equiv=Content-Type content="text/html; charset=iso-8859-
1">

<STYLE type=text/css>@import URL("estilos.css");</STYLE>

<META content="youreditor" name=GENERATOR>

<META content="Marcellux-2003" name=AUTHOR>

</HEAD>

<BODY >

<TABLE   border=2>

<TR align=middle><TD height=14 borderColorDark=green
borderColorLight=lightgreen><img border="0" src="logofacu-ch.gif"
width="40" height="47"></TD>

<TD height=21><p align="center"><b><font size="1" face="Arial"
color="#800000">Subject Name</font></b></p></TD>

<TD><FONT><a target="mainframe" href="nosotros.htm"> About
us</a></FONT></TD>
```

```
<TD><FONT><a target="mainframe" href="GUIDE">Exercises
Guide</a></FONT></TD>

<TD><FONT><a target="menu" href="menuteo.htm">Exercises for
Theory</a></FONT></TD>

<TD><font><a target="mainframe" href="Exercises.htm"> Exercises with
solutions included</a></font></TD>

<TD ><FONT><a target="_top"
href="http://www.econ.uba.ar/www/departamentos/sistemas/plan97/tecn_
informac/seoane/seoane/index.htm"> Academic
Rules</a></FONT></TD>

<TD ><FONT><a target="mainframe" href="program.htm"> Contents of
the subject</a></FONT></TD>

<TD> <FONT><a target="mainframe" href="survey.htm"> Survey
</a></FONT> </TD>

</TR></TABLE><BR></BODY></HTML>
```

instru.htm.

SFT Module

You can download the source code from
http://www5.domaindlx.com/mgbosq/instru.htm

Select the option "view source code" in your explorer and then copy &
paste the code to your computer.

```
<HTML><HEAD>
<META http-equiv=Content-Type content="text/html; charset=windows-
1252">
<META content="youreditor" name=GENERATOR>
<STYLE type=text/css>@import URL("innercnrt.css");</STYLE>
</HEAD><BODY>

<TABLE> <TR> <TD>How to fill the form</TD></TR>
 <TR><TD>
   Alter you  have filled the form, you have to send it pressing the button
that is located at the end of the page. This will add your personal data to
the internal database of the course.
</TD></TR></TABLE></BODY></HTML>
```

SQM Module

It opens a database and a recordset.

```
Set DB1 = Server.CreateObject("ADODB.Connection")
Dri="DRIVER=Microsoft Access Driver (*.mdb);DBQ="
Dri= Dri & Server.MapPath("dbempremovil.mdb")
DB1.Open Dri

Set RS1 = Server.CreateObject("ADODB.Recordset")
TQuery="SELECT * FROM Students  WHERE [name]='smith'
ORDER BY [name]"
RS1.Open TQuery, DB1
```

LoadStudent.asp

It opens a database and a recordset to show the contents of the databese.

```
<% studentID      =Request.Form("ID") %>
<% studentname    =Request.Form("name") %>
<% studentad=Request.Form("address") %>
<% studentage     =Request.Form("age") %>
<% studentemail   =Request.Form("email") %>


<% if studentID=null then %>
<FORM ACTION="loadstudent.asp" NAME="formpmc"
METHOD="POST" target=mainframe>
<p><font size="1">Introduce Student ID:</font></p>
```

```
<INPUT TYPE="TEXT" NAME="ID"       VALUE="" >
<INPUT TYPE="TEXT" NAME="name"     VALUE="" >
<INPUT TYPE="TEXT" NAME="address"  VALUE="" >
<INPUT TYPE="TEXT" NAME="age"      VALUE="" >
<INPUT TYPE="TEXT" NAME="email"    VALUE="" >

<INPUT TYPE="SUBMIT" NAME="submit1" VALUE="Press Here
to Submit" >
<INPUT TYPE="RESET"  NAME="Reset1" VALUE="Reset" >

<% else %>

Initial= " , "

Final= " ', "

StudentID      = "( ' "   & studentID & final

Studentname    =initial & studentID & final

Studentad      =initial & studentad & final

Studentage     =initial & studentage & final

Studentemail   =initial & studentemail & " ' )"

Allstudents= studentID & studentname & studentad & studentage &
studentmail

X= " INSERT INTO students  (ID,name,address,age,e-mail)  VALUES "

SQL=X & Allstudents

xct=BD1.Execute SQL

%><a href="index.html>Insertion Done. Press here to continue</a><%
<% end if %>
```

ModifyStudent.asp

It opens a database and a recordset to change the values of a record that was already created .

```
<% studentID      =Request.Form("ID") %>
<% studentname    =Request.Form("name") %>
<% studentad=Request.Form("address") %>
<% studentage      =Request.Form("age") %>
<% studentemail    =Request.Form("email") %>


<% if studentID=null then %>
<FORM ACTION="modifystudent.asp" NAME="formpmc"
METHOD="POST" target=mainframe>
<p><font size="1">Introduce Student ID:</font></p>

<INPUT TYPE="TEXT" NAME="ID"        VALUE="" >
<INPUT TYPE="TEXT" NAME="name"      VALUE="" >
<INPUT TYPE="TEXT" NAME="address"  VALUE="" >
<INPUT TYPE="TEXT" NAME="age"        VALUE="" >
<INPUT TYPE="TEXT" NAME="email"      VALUE="" >

<INPUT TYPE="SUBMIT" NAME="submit1" VALUE="Press Here
to Submit" >
<INPUT TYPE="RESET"  NAME="Reset1" VALUE="Reset" >

<% else %>

<%
Set DB1 = Server.CreateObject("ADODB.Connection")
Dri="DRIVER=Microsoft Access Driver (*.mdb);DBQ="
Dri= Dri & Server.MapPath("dbempremovil.mdb")
DB1.Open Dri
```

```
Set RS1 = Server.CreateObject("ADODB.Recordset")
TQuery="SELECT * FROM Students  WHERE [ID]=" &
Request.Form("ID") & "ORDER BY [name]"
RS1.Open TQuery, DB1
%>

SQL="UPDATE students SET name='" & Request.Form("Studentname")
& "'  WHERE ID=" & Request.form("StudentID")


xct=BD1.Execute SQL

%><a href="index.html>Modification Done. Press here to
continue</a><%
<% end if %>

<% end if %>
```

EraseStudent.asp

It opens a database and a recordset to erase one or more records.

```
<% studentID=Request.Form("ID") %>

<% if studentID=null then %>
<FORM ACTION="students.asp" NAME="formpmc"
METHOD="POST" target=mainframe>
<p><font size="1">Introduce Student ID:</font></p>
<INPUT TYPE="TEXT" NAME="ID" VALUE="" >
<INPUT TYPE="SUBMIT" NAME="submit1" VALUE="Press Here
to Submit" >
<INPUT TYPE="RESET"  NAME="Reset1" VALUE="Reset" >
```

```
<% else %>
<%
Set DB1 = Server.CreateObject("ADODB.Connection")
Dri="DRIVER=Microsoft Access Driver (*.mdb);DBQ="
Dri= Dri & Server.MapPath("dbempremovil.mdb")
DB1.Open Dri

Set RS1 = Server.CreateObject("ADODB.Recordset")
TQuery="SELECT * FROM Students  WHERE [ID]=" & studentID "
RS1.Open TQuery, DB1
%>
<% SQL="DELETE FROM Students WHERE [ID]='" & StudentID &
"'"

xct=BD1.Execute SQL

%><a href="index.html>The record has been erased. Press here to
continue</a><%


<% end if %>
```

ABOUT THE AUTHOR

Dr. Marcelo Bosque (L.A.) is graduated from University of Buenos Aires, where he teaches. He is also a visual artist, and writes scientific and technical books.

0-595-27176-6